Jesse Fink was born in London in 1973. He is best known as a sportswriter for the TV networks Fox Sports, ESPN STAR Sports and SBS, and has provided opinion for or been quoted as a commentator in other media outlets such as CNN, BBC Sport, Al Jazeera and the *Wall Street Journal.* Between 2006 and 2011 Fink was the most read online soccer columnist in Australia.

He has also contributed stories to publications such as *Inside Sport, Dazed & Confused, Jakarta Globe, marie claire* and *Cosmopolitan.*

In 2003 he was nominated for a Walkley Award for print journalism and in 2007 released his first book, *15 Days in June: How Australia Became a Football Nation.*

He lives in Sydney, Australia.

LAID BARE

JESSE FINK

Published in Australia and New Zealand in 2012
by Hachette Australia
(an imprint of Hachette Australia Pty Limited)
Level 17, 207 Kent Street, Sydney NSW 2000
www.hachette.com.au

10 9 8 7 6 5 4 3 2 1

Copyright © Jesse Fink 2012

This book is copyright. Apart from any fair dealing for the purposes of private study, research, criticism or review permitted under the *Copyright Act 1968*, no part may be stored or reproduced by any process without prior written permission. Enquiries should be made to the publisher.

National Library of Australia
Cataloguing-in-Publication data

Fink, Jesse, 1973–

    Laid Bare: one man's story of sex, love
    and other disorders / Jesse Fink.

    9780733629044 (pbk.)

    Fink, Jesse, 1973–
    Interpersonal relations.
    Man – woman relationships.

920.71

Cover design by Christabella Designs
Cover photograph courtesy of Getty Images
Author photograph by Grace Cassio
Typeset in Sabon by Kirby Jones
Printed in Australia by Griffin Press, Adelaide, an Accredited ISO AS/NZS 4001:2004 Environmental Management Systems printer

The paper this book is printed on is certified against the Forest Stewardship Council® Standards. Griffin Press holds FSC chain of custody certification SGS-COC-005088. FSC promotes environmentally responsible, socially beneficial and economically viable management of the world's forests.

To my daughter, my hero

In the immortal words of Bon Scott, 'The following is a true story. Only the names have been changed … to protect the guilty.' As well as a few identifying personal characteristics, occupations, locations …

CONTENTS

AUTHOR'S NOTE   xiii

Chapter 1 **THE RUPTURE**   1

Chapter 2 **THE CHOKE**   19

Chapter 3 **A DRESSING SHED WITH A COFFEE DECK**   34

Chapter 4 **EATING OUT**   54

Chapter 5 **DIVORCED FATHERS AND DAUGHTERS ALL-STARS**   71

Chapter 6 **TURBULENCE ADDICTION**   91

Chapter 7 **BAD FATHER**   105

Chapter 8 **SMALL WORLD**   125

Chapter 9 **WHORING BY DEGREES**   142

Chapter 10 **THE BUCK'S NIGHT**   162

Chapter 11 **LIFE'S FURNITURE**   178

Chapter 12 **ALL PLAYED OUT**   194

Chapter 13 **INTO THE UNKNOWN**   218

Chapter 14 **A LITTLE PATIENCE**   243

Chapter 15 **LET THE RIGHT ONE IN**   268

Chapter 16 **BETTER MAN**   293

SOUNDTRACK   299

ACKNOWLEDGMENTS   302

'As love is an emotional glimpse of eternity, one can't help half-believing that genuine love will last forever.'
– *Stephen Vizinczey*

AUTHOR'S NOTE

There are roughly 50,000 divorces and 70,000 separations each year in Australia and those figures are high, just as they are in the United States, the United Kingdom, across Europe and in other countries around the world.

Love and relationships are under siege.

Many relationships that start out passionately end in acrimony, heartache and recrimination. My first marriage, which lasted a decade from introduction to separation, was one of them and much of *Laid Bare* is the story (from my point of view, at least) of that divorce and an attempt to document the complex cycle of feelings husbands and fathers go through when they get their hearts broken and watch their families disintegrate around them.

It's also a cautionary tale of how many men use online-dating sites as vagina catalogues, an insight into what those same men look for in women and my attempt to show that a lot of us, including 'bad boys', are much more emotional and sensitive than we might otherwise let on. Men want love. We just want a whole bunch of other things too.

Not everything I say is going to sit well with everybody, but that's something I am used to, having made some of my reputation as a sportswriter who was paid to ruffle feathers. You might agree with all of it. You may find it completely abhorrent and me personally offensive. So be it. I have written *Laid Bare* as honestly as I can to throw a light not just on what I see as some of society's shortcomings but also on my own. I have plenty.

My sincere hope is this book gets people talking about what we're all doing when it comes to love and whether there are better ways to go about having, enjoying and maintaining relationships.

As Ronnie James Dio sang, and I'm a firm believer in this, 'Love is all.'

Jesse Fink
Darlinghurst,
September 2012

CHAPTER 1

THE RUPTURE

TRACK 1 'Losin' End', The Doobie Brothers, *Takin' It to the Streets* (1976)

There are moments in life that deliver a jolt, where time stands still, which make you confront who you are, why you're here, what it is you're doing and whatever the hell it is you're going to do next.

This was one of them, my erect cock resting on the chin of one of the most famous women in Australia. Patricia had been on the cover of numerous women's magazines.

'Come in my mouth,' she said.

It had only taken thousands of dollars in psychotherapy, prescription drugs, domestic and international airfares, crates of wine, hundreds of dates, innumerable screws, being tied up, sucked off, smacked, rimmed, trying to make myself feel *alive* any which way I could, but it finally dawned on me at that exact moment.

I was okay.

I didn't need to align my chakras or go to a meditation retreat in the bush or stand around a campfire sharing my story with other men in crisis or see another goddamn doctor. By doing what this crooked-lipped sylph was asking, I was finally doing what friends and family had wanted me to do all along.

I was 'moving on'.

At this very point in time, how could I want anything more? Wasn't this what every man wanted? Lived for? Doing to a beautiful woman what most women, beautiful or otherwise, weren't exactly offering up on a plate for their boyfriends or husbands, let alone a random internet fuck in a $10 million home by Sydney Harbour on a school night?

Everything that had come before suddenly didn't matter. Straddling Patricia's face, I looked out through the window, past the expensive, thick, red velvet drapes and the immaculate green lawn and elaborate water feature, to the dark cove where white yachts were bobbing in the moonlight.

How did I get here?

I closed my eyes, unloaded and, like the Eddie Van Halen keyboard solo in 'Jump' playing out in my head, a new part

THE RUPTURE

of my life began: the part where I didn't have to look back with regret anymore.

* * *

Perhaps the more relevant question is not how I'd got there but why had it taken so long. It was 2010 and I'd been divorced a couple of years. I was 37, at my physical peak and reasonably attractive to most women I met in the course of my working day. I was a sportswriter with a bunch of online opinion columns, a couple in Australia, another overseas and altogether making enough money to get by without actually doing much work at all.

Years before I'd stumbled by accident on the life I'd always wanted when I'd got drunk in a Hamburg nightclub with a balding, overweight English producer called Will who worked for Fox Sports, a pay-TV channel in Australia. Red cheeked, sweaty and missing his shirt, he'd come down from dancing on a podium, walked up to the bar where I was resting my elbows alongside a shot of vodka, thrown an arm around me and straight up offered me a job.

'Hey, grumpy. I've got a proposition for you,' he said. 'Write me a column about soccer. I'll pay you for an hour's work what you make in a day.'

At the time I was writing for and editing Australia's longest-running sports magazine, *Inside Sport*, and the Socceroos, Australia's men's team, had just qualified for Germany 2006, their first appearance at a World Cup since 1974. This had occasioned the German government, in their infinite wisdom, to pay for me, Will and a bunch of other ingrate journos to go around the country for ten days – no expense spared – in the hope we'd write positive things.

Naturally, rather than soberly reading plaques at war memorials we spent most of those ten days off our faces in beer halls and pumping discotheques. The writer from *Vogue* even pissed in a dustbin by the elevator doors of a hotel in Düsseldorf. With the money on offer and Will's level of intoxication, it was a no-brainer. I accepted. When we'd sobered up and got back home Will made it happen and the column was a hit. I never looked back.

The job set me free. After years of toiling as an underpaid, overworked editor of books and magazines, I was finally unencumbered and relatively unstressed. With a laptop and the wonder of wireless technology, I could write anywhere. The beach. The park. The pool. Any number of café tables. Bars. Airport lounges. Hotel rooms. My bed. Other people's beds.

'The web,' said Will, 'is where it's at.' And he was right. For me it was that and more. It was freedom.

THE RUPTURE

The column, called 'Half-Time Orange', didn't demand much of my time. Typically by midmorning each day of the week I would come up with something controversial to say about scumbag FIFA executive committee members or an inept national-team coach or federation official, bang out 500 or 600 furious words designed to piss off the maximum amount of people, send it off to Will and his team of editors and then forget all about it. The comments and hits rolled in. When I did piles of research or picked topics that were important but not populist, the comments and hits dried up. It suited my employers that I became, in effect, a 'shock jock'.

After a year at Fox, I switched networks, to SBS, one of Australia's two public broadcasters and the rights holder of the World Cup, increasing my reach. When Will followed me to SBS soon afterwards, I was offered another column called 'The Finktank' with the brief to write about anything I liked. There was talk of me even co-hosting an online show with one of SBS's female stars.

But career progression didn't interest me so much at that point in my life. What I was really interested in, to be frank, was my sex life. I had sex with lots of women in all kinds of places and the work allowed me to fuck girls anywhere. It was a double life of sorts but I was hooked.

* * *

LAID BARE

A wry but concerned friend once joked that my only weaknesses were 'pussy and cheesecake' and to others, including my family, it might well have looked that way. In truth, though, I was no bounder and these preoccupations were only recent. I believed in love.

I was searching for it because I'd lost it. Or rather, her. Lara. My wife and the mother of my gorgeous, copper-haired three-year-old daughter, Evie.

A gifted singer who'd turned her back on a major-label contract and potential pop stardom because she didn't like the way she was being packaged by her record company, Lara was the most physically enthralling woman I'd ever met. Five foot six, 25 years old, long dirty-blonde hair, coquettish eyes, high cheekbones, a smile wider than Julia Roberts's and, crucially, for they were always talking points, tits as heavy and perfectly formed as Monica Bellucci's. We fucked constantly. While her magnetism and force of personality could start parties when she walked into a room, equally she possessed such a lack of self-consciousness as to be able to walk down to the supermarket in her pyjamas and ugg boots. Importantly, she was also bright, generous, doting, affectionate and sensitive. All of which, in my eyes, made her the perfect wife. I loved her and lusted after her with everything I had, and it was a lot.

Yet after ten years of being together, eight married, three as parents, she left me. 'I love you but I'm not *in love* with you' were her exact words that awful autumn day in 2007. I had never even contemplated hearing them – Lara was my best friend, my soul mate – but they came, forcefully and with no room for negotiation, as we sat on the end of our bed in Enfield, a suburb in the inner west of Sydney. Her declaration came two weeks before I was due to release my first book, a non-fiction work about Australian soccer, based in part on a trip Lara, Evie and I had made together as a family to France and Germany to follow the Socceroos at the World Cup. It even had a dedication to her. It couldn't be removed.

Not quite believing what I'd just heard, I asked her to stay until the launch so I could hold myself together. She agreed.

Standing before a room of hundreds of my friends, family, work colleagues and celebrities, including Lara (who was there to show her 'support'), and trying to muster up the will to smile, make jokes and enjoy the moment, my heart felt like it had been cut in half with a meat cleaver and left to drain, twitching but still beating, on a chopping block. It was like I'd come to celebrate my own death.

I hadn't seen any of it coming. I considered myself to be smart, well read and a good conversationalist. I had interesting friends and exotic social networks. I adored my wife. I'd never cheated on her. I was, I thought, safe from such a calamity. We'd had problems beyond our control, not least her mother's husband dropping dead while mowing the back lawn of their rented home. Because he'd been the breadwinner, they'd saved very little and she couldn't drive, it left us no option but to invite Lara's mother to move in with us while she grieved. (She stayed more than six months, slept in our living room and was there in her dressing gown and slippers clutching a pack of smokes when we separated.) Yet every relationship faces challenges. This wasn't supposed to happen. Not to *me*.

How had I managed to miss it?

* * *

Many men make this mistake or at least variations of it at one time or another. It's just that some of us twig before it's too late. Or get the opportunity to talk through problems and work things out with our partners before succumbing to the inevitable split. I didn't get either luxury. It was final. Over. Done. As quick and effective as a guillotine.

It took the rupture of Lara's leaving, the separation and the subsequent fast-tracked divorce (I got the full treatment 12 months later: sheriffs at the door with pepper spray on their belts and court papers in their fists) for me to confront what I had become. And that was a fat fuck-up who, deep in the midst of a decade-long relationship, had somehow lost his way, eating tubs of Ben & Jerry's ice cream in front of *Jerry Springer* at two in the morning.

Begrudgingly, but much later, I even came to admit my ex-wife might have been right to leave me. Physically, I wasn't in the least bit attractive or fuckable. I was pasty. Had two chins and man tits. A bowling ball for a head. I dressed badly. My gut was so large I couldn't even see my dick when I looked down. I hadn't been that way when we'd first met. I convinced myself I was too busy writing my book to exercise but that was only a small part of the story. I was a disappointment to myself and must have been a frightful sight to Lara, especially naked.

It wasn't like my personality was exactly making up for it either. For years I'd been afflicted with major depression and a particularly nasty variant of obsessive-compulsive disorder called 'Pure-O' or purely obsessional OCD, which had rendered me completely useless for a large part of the final years of our marriage.

OCD. The Wagnerian opera of headfucks. I was bombarded around the clock by disturbing thoughts. Every minute of every hour. The worst kind of thoughts imaginable. And I didn't know where they were coming from, why I was having them or how to stop them. Antidepressants didn't help. Whatever my doctors prescribed – Prozac, Paxil, Zoloft and the rest of a lucky dip of selective serotonin reuptake inhibitors (SSRIs) – just made me fatter and more miserable. Cognitive behaviour therapy with some of the best psychiatrists in the country couldn't unlock the problem. No matter how much I wanted to get out of the black hole I was in, I didn't know how. I physically and emotionally existed for Lara and wanted to be there for her, but rarely was.

For a long time my wife tried to understand what I was going through and be there for me, and I put her through a lot, telling her frankly what was plaguing me and seeking her reassurance that I wasn't going mad, but I don't think she ever quite *got* it. I tried to give her books to read, but they went unopened. Eventually, when a doctor suggested that in fact she might be depressed too and wrote her a prescription for Prozac, she'd had enough.

Lara told me the only thing that made her unhappy was me. She was going to let me claw out of this trough all by myself and get back what was left of her own life. Of course I didn't agree with her decision – I felt she had given up on us as couple and the three of us as a family when I needed her most – but there was nothing I could do about it. And looking back, that was probably the key issue. I needed her too much. But I saw none of that then.

What I could do, though, was become the man I used to be and was capable of being once more – not just to resuscitate my self-esteem but to stand a chance of ever having a meaningful relationship again, with Lara or anyone else. And late at night for weeks and months after the separation, feeling the most alone I'd ever felt in my life, my wife, best friend, family, pet, identity, physical condition, mental health, dream of siblings for Evie and storybook future wrested away from me by a confluence of self-hate, bad luck, fate, obsessional thinking and reawakened female needs, winning Lara back was all I could think about.

Of course, I was about to go absolutely the wrong way about it. I was just another stupid male, after all.

* * *

When an old girlfriend alerted me to a studio that had just been listed for rent in the inner-city suburb of Darlinghurst, it seemed as good a place as any to get myself sorted. A few months had passed. Lara had moved to an undisclosed address in Haberfield, not far from Enfield. I had been staying at my mother Sal's house in Leichhardt, a suburb away, but the arrangement wasn't working for anybody.

Though she dressed like a car crash between Vivienne Westwood and Winnie Mandela and decorated her house with junk salvaged from the side of the road, Sal, a retired glass artist, had made a substantial fortune in real estate by 'following the ferals' up and down the east coast of Australia. Her hard and fast rule: wherever the artistic types went, the yuppies and their money followed. She'd done particularly well out of the 'Bs' – Birchgrove, Balmain, Broken Head, Belongil, Byron Bay and Bundeena – which had seen her amass millions while maintaining the carefully cultivated appearance of a batshit-crazy eccentric.

My mother had taken me in when my wife had dropped her bomb and was doing her best to help me through a crisis she said she'd seen coming long ago. But there was a reason I'd moved out 15 years before: we weren't meant to live together. Under the same roof, and in my fragile emotional state, she might as well have been a gorgon and not the woman who'd brought me into the world. We fought terribly over who was to blame for the separation. Sal thought I'd neglected Lara. I had, but I couldn't admit that then and I sure as hell didn't need to hear that from my own mother. When I walked in on her calling me a 'cunt' on the phone to Lara, it was time to go. There are some things a son should never hear.

The east had a reputation for being expensive, superficial, narcissistic and class driven and in many ways the reputation was well earned. It was a part of town where old-school gangsters and their halfwit progeny were celebrities; where western suburbs wog boys blown up on steroids would try their luck with glacial private-school blondes at nightclubs on weekends; where gymnasiums saw more action in the men's toilets than on the weights floor; where pretty women would rent themselves as party dates to rich but socially inept entrepreneurs for $2000-a-week allowances; where the Sunday social pages attracted more readers than the headline news; where real estate, clothing labels, model girlfriends and ready access to cocaine and the Facebook walls of plastic surgeons were the marks of one's status in the unspoken but inextricable nexus of beach, café, bar and club. 'North Bondi relationships', where two attractive but vacant people paired off for no other reason than to look good together, were de rigueur.

Having grown up in the old wharfies' suburb of Balmain, spending most of my formative years in and around the more grounded inner west, the east was everything I despised but it was just what I needed. I would even come to love it. I wanted something new; to disappear; to have the time and space to process what had happened to me and do whatever it was going to take to get my shit together enough to be at least remotely palatable to Lara on the few occasions we came together.

And, if the opportunity arose, to other women.

The idea of being with anyone else, however, was completely alien to me at that time. All through my marriage I'd been so in love with Lara, so sexually satisfied and so content with the life we had that I'd never had to stray. I hadn't even so much as looked at another woman; I hadn't had to.

Except for one.

Her name was Brooke and I'd met her when I was at *Inside Sport*. She worked for another magazine on another floor, and at 24 was like a mirror image of Lara ten years before. I was helplessly attracted to her.

One afternoon early in 2007, months before the separation, she invited me to a picnic at a cricket oval near where we worked on Sydney's north shore.

I sat there longing to touch this identikit of my wife as a younger woman. The tension was unbearable. I had the urge to lean over, kiss Brooke's neck and twirl a strand of her blonde hair around one of my fingers in the bright winter sun. It was like a 1970s Flake commercial. She was breathtaking. But the situation was also fundamentally dumb.

What turned me on about Brooke was that she reminded me of the woman I was already married to, the only woman I'd ever loved, who I was starting to have trouble connecting with at home. So I went back to Enfield and told Lara what had happened: I'd been tempted for the first time in all our years together but I'd had an epiphany and had come to realise just how important she was to me; my flirtation with this young girl had actually made our marriage stronger.

THE RUPTURE

I was being as honest as I could be and was convinced that I was doing the right thing by our relationship. On reflection, though, it was a grave mistake. I had just told my wife I'd been tempted by another woman. I'd even spent time alone with her. Lara said it was all perfectly fine and she appreciated my honesty but she hadn't bought it. And I'd effectively given her a green light to flirt with other people.

After that we grew even more distant. Lara spent more time with her friends, playing gigs with her band, going out to pubs and clubs and not coming home till the early hours of the morning. Rather than go with her, I stayed at home to look after Evie. Eventually she told me she was unhappy and wanted us to try counselling. I agreed to it but underestimated the depth of her dissatisfaction. When we came out of a session and she told me she loved me even though she clearly remained miserable, I took it as insurance that nothing would ever happen to us. I eased off when I should have been making the biggest effort of my life to save what we still had.

Blithely, while we were stuck in gridlock traffic on Parramatta Road one afternoon after another gruelling counselling session, I even snapped that she could walk away if she was going to stay so unhappy.

'If you really feel that way, Lara, then you should leave,' I said. 'I don't ever want you to be unhappy.'

What I was trying to say in my typically cocked-up fashion was that I loved her so much that I would never stand in the way of her happiness. But what she heard and took in was something else altogether.

* * *

I didn't have to wait long for confirmation that we were in deep trouble. Lara came home late one night from a day with her friends at a horseracing carnival, highly intoxicated and wanting action. I was in bed after a day of writing my book. She climbed on top of me, still in her fascinator, and fucked me like I was someone else. Her eyes were distant and wouldn't meet mine. When it was over, I started crying. Spontaneous tears. Lara started crying too.

'I'm sorry, darling,' she said, hugging me. 'I don't know what's going on with me.' She looked deeply sad.

'Is there someone else, Lara? Tell me the truth.'

'No.'

I didn't believe her but we pressed ourselves together tightly, saying nothing for what felt like hours. Just holding each other as closely as we could.

I didn't get any sleep that night. I had no idea what was going through her head.

THE RUPTURE

* * *

For months after the separation I was telling any woman I'd meet this story. They looked at me with sympathy. They said it was clear there was another man involved and, in the event there wasn't, that night of unpleasant sex had been the beginning of the end.

They were wrong. It had been over well before then but I had allowed myself to suspend all my instinct for panic and think that with the counselling we were going to be alright; that the whole point of marriage was getting through critical situations, emotional, financial or otherwise, and emerging out the other end with a relationship that was even stronger for the experience.

But it was irrelevant what I thought if Lara didn't see it that way. And she didn't. She was resolved. Committed to leaving me and starting over again.

As we sat on that bed in Enfield, she told me she'd left our relationship long ago, an 'oppressive weight' was off her shoulders and she wasn't coming back.

I was, in her eyes, controlling, insecure, needy and possessive. (Which was probably true, given I'd been convinced for years that she wasn't going to stick around when I remained so sick.) I required too much looking after. Her love for me had turned into a duty. She worried too much about me. I'd worn her down. She wanted lightness, not the darkness I emanated. She was going to make a new life and she didn't want me to know where she was going with Evie.

Or, naturally, the name of the man she was now with. But I'd find out both soon enough.

CHAPTER 2

THE CHOKE

TRACK 2 'Lyin' Eyes', Eagles,
One of These Nights (1975)

'Who the *fuck* are you?'

It was all I could think to say while standing motionless in the doorway of the homewares shop Lara worked in. We'd been separated a matter of weeks. I'd dropped by unannounced to ask about some missing luggage I needed for a work trip to Thailand, where the Asian Cup, Asia's biggest soccer tournament, was about to kick off. I walked in on an older guy I didn't know kissing her while reaching across the front counter. I felt like I'd been shot between the eyes.

On seeing me he'd fled, but I'd got enough of a look at him to see that he had grey hair and a ponytail, was taller than me and wore a leather jacket. A rocker.

My wife's reaction was unusual. She laughed.

'It's really not what you think, Jesse,' she said, trying to make light of the situation.

'A man was *kissing* you, Lara.'

'He's just a guy who's been helping me move.'

'Lara.'

I stepped forward, getting as close to her as I could. She tried walking away. She was very nervous.

'He put up a brushwood fence for me. He came by to give me a present and leaned over and kissed me and you walked in. It was bad timing.'

'What's his name?' I could feel myself trembling.

'It doesn't matter.'

'Tell me his fucking *name*, Lara!' My whole body was shaking now.

'Tim. His name is Tim. Now you have to go. I have to work.'

But I couldn't so much as put one foot in front of the other. I was stunned. Struggling to get the words out.

'*Lara.*'

I reached for my wife's shoulders, took her face in my hands and pulled it toward mine. Her eyes gave nothing to me; they were dead, opaque, like a pet that had just been put to sleep. She said nothing and pushed me away. The only woman I'd ever loved, the mother of my child, seemed like someone I didn't even know. I sat on a milk crate outside the back door of the shop and wept for well over an hour. I don't think I'd ever cried so much in my life.

Lara rang my father, Alby, to come and collect me. When he arrived he assured me it wasn't what it seemed, that I had to give her time and space. He put me in his car and took me home. But it *was* what it seemed. Lara called later that day and said she wanted a divorce.

On hearing that, after holding myself together as best as I could, I fell apart completely.

Alby wasn't going to leave me on my own. He booked a last-minute ticket for himself and we flew to Bangkok together. For ten days I managed not to kill myself. But I did my best.

One night in Sukhumvit I drank so much whisky I passed out on the dance floor of a nightclub. Miraculously I woke up back at my hotel, my kidneys and wallet intact, with Alby holding up my head and wiping vomit off my shirt.

'My boy, *why* do you do this to yourself?'

* * *

It seemed like a good idea.

If Lara wasn't going to tell me where she was living with Evie, I'd get in my car and drive around Haberfield, up and down every street and lane, looking for some brushwood.

After five hours I couldn't find anything that looked like the kind of place where Lara would live. Nothing about the houses I saw with brushwood suggested she was living there. No fairy lights. No Moroccan glazed pots. No cacti. No kid's bicycle. No dog. I returned back to my bedsit, disconsolate.

Why couldn't she understand that I wanted to know where my daughter was living? Couldn't she see the pain I was in? More than anything, why didn't she want *me*, her husband, if there was nothing to the shop incident? I was the man who truly loved her. Not him. This *creep*. I was the one cut off from everything that meant anything to me. The one living the half of a whole. I wanted the whole again but didn't know how it would ever come back or even know where to start to look for it.

The powerlessness I felt was overwhelming. The urge that followed came as naturally as breathing.

I opened a drawer in the kitchen, took out a steak knife, sat down at the table by the one window in the dismal few square metres I now called home and pressed the tip of the blade down on the big vein on my left wrist. I had an impulse to plunge it deep into my skin. I could see the blood gushing up into my face like a burst pipe to join the tears streaming down my cheeks. But as I traced the outlines of my veins with the metal, leaving a long red trail of broken skin, I knew killing myself was a cop-out. Even though I wanted to release the torment inside me, a searing, terrible pain I had never known in my life before, I couldn't do it to Evie. I couldn't do it to myself. To give in now would hurt everyone, including Lara. I put the knife down and began sobbing, rocking with grief.

I don't know how long I sat there. Hours. But eventually I got up and went to bed, eating a handful of pills. I think I slept for about three days. Waking up was just too painful.

* * *

The mystery of where Lara was living was solved a week later when I picked up my daughter from day care. My custody arrangement with Lara was 50:50. Straight down the middle. Wednesday to Friday one week. Wednesday to Sunday the next. For no good reason, I took a different route home.

'Dad, that's our house!' Evie said suddenly as we drove up a street I was sure I had clocked on my failed brushwood reconnaissance. How had I not noticed it? The fence was there, all right, out the rear of the house, backing on to a laneway. Evie told me she lived in this part. The front part on the other street was someone else's place. There were two self-contained flats at the one address. I stepped out of my car and called out my dog Bosco's name. He barked. I got back inside. Evie, strapped into her booster seat, beamed at me. I told her not to tell her mum that I knew where she lived. That it was a secret between her and me.

Around this time Lara was preparing to go into hospital to have minor day surgery. I thought it was a good opportunity for me to have some contact and be there for her, so I offered to drive her to the hospital and then pick her up when it was over. She didn't go for it, saying that her boss at the shop had already volunteered. I was gutted, but promised I'd take care of Evie while she was recovering.

That evening, I was lying back in my bed with Evie.

We were chatting away, just a normal father–daughter talk about school and friends and movies and animals, when apropos of nothing my little girl turned and said, excitedly: 'Daddy, Mummy's sleeping with a man tonight!'

Out of the mouths of babes. She blurted it out like she thought it would make me happy. Her tiny face had lit up, totally oblivious to the import of what she was telling me; completely unaware of the chain of events it would precipitate.

'Evie, what does the man look like? Does he have grey hair and a ponytail?'

'Yes, Daddy.'

'Does he wear a leather jacket?'

'Yes.'

'And you've met him?'

'Yes.'

'What kind of car does he drive?'

'An old green one.'

'Is his name Tim?'

'No, Daddy. His name's David.'

My nerves were sparking like shorted wires. I couldn't think straight. I told Evie to get dressed. She had to come with me. I couldn't leave her at home alone. And there was no question of me not going.

* * *

When I turned into Lara's street a vintage 1960s Hillman Minx the colour of a jade tea set was parked outside her place. The side gate, the only access to the flat, was locked. I buzzed. There was no answer. I buzzed once more. Again, no answer. But I could hear noise coming from inside. Music was turned down. There was movement. Murmuring. No one was coming to the door. Whoever this man was – Tim or David – he was in there with my wife.

The gate was high but not high enough to prevent me from climbing over.

'Evie, don't move.'

Once I'd jumped down to the other side, I undid the latch. I took my daughter's hand. I should have backed away, for Evie's sake, but I didn't. I was like an elephant in musth. Nothing was going to stop me confronting this man.

I got to the back door and bashed it hard. I yelled at Lara to let me in. She could hear that Evie was with me. There was the sound of a deadbolt being turned. Bursting in, I barely even looked in her direction. She was a blur. Lara grabbed Evie and stepped back into the kitchen, clutching her tightly.

'Right, where is he?'

'Go home,' she said. 'Jesse, *please*. Go home!'

I could see a door at the back of the flat was locked. There were no other unopened doors, just this one. He had to be behind that locked door. I moved forward, feeling more scared than at any time in my life, but purposeful. Indestructible. The avenging hero.

The moment my hand touched the doorknob I got knocked back hard. No exchange of words. No confrontation like the scenario I'd been playing in my head on the drive there. Beyond a flash of salt and pepper, I didn't even see his face. There was just a forearm. And it was on my throat. My wife's lover was choking me. I tried pulling at his ponytail but I couldn't swivel around to get any purchase. He had me from behind and my swinging arms were just finding air. I was turning blue. My eyeballs were going to pop. I tried to tell Lara to stop him, but I couldn't speak. All I could hear was a sound-effects reel of screams and tears. My wife's and my child's.

And then I blacked out.

I came to in a garden bed outside, face down in the dirt. My glasses were smashed. The door to the flat was slammed shut. Lara and Evie were inside and not about to come out. I got up and went to the door, hammering it with my fists and unleashing a torrent of abuse.

'You unspeakable piece of *SHIT*! How could you come between a *FAMILY* like this? How the *FUCK* do you sleep at night? She's the mother of my *CHILD*! They're my family. My *FAMILY*! You fucking *CUNT*. You low dog. You despicable fucking *DOG*!'

My face was up against the doorframe like Jack Nicholson in *The Shining*. If I'd had an axe I would have torn it apart. Evie must have been terrified. The guilt would come later.

Lara was the only one to speak.

'Jesse, I've called the police. And your mother.'

I continued yelling some more, just words and spittle, until I had expended all my fury. There was nothing else to say. Nothing left inside me. What was going to change anything now or make me come out of this looking any good? There was silence inside the house. Only the neighbourhood dogs were paying me any notice, an impromptu canine orchestra having formed in response to the ruckus. I slumped on a sandstone wall leading down to the garden and waited for the cavalry to arrive. It was past midnight.

Sal embraced me and didn't try to sugarcoat it.

'At least you know now, son,' she said, standing over me like a badged detective in a forensic crime drama. 'I've called an ambulance. I think you need it.'

The ambulance driver asked me to come sit with him in the front seat of his vehicle and to shut the door behind me. I did as he asked. I wanted to die.

'I could give you something right now, but I'm not going to,' he said, fixing me straight in the eye. He was about 40, with a shaved head and a trimmed goatee. 'I know what you're going through, mate. I've been there myself. I wanted to shoot the cunt *dead*. Kill him. I was ready to do it. I had the gun and all. I was ready to go to jail. But I didn't do it. Trust me, you'll look back on this one day and it won't mean anything to you at all. You move on. You will get a new wife, a new family, a new life. It will just be a memory, mate. You are going to be okay. You don't need anything from me tonight. You just need to go home and rest. Put it behind you.'

They were the most comforting words I had heard from anyone since Lara had walked out, from the least expected quarter and from a man whose occupation was all about dealing with stress and people in pain. He knew what he was talking about.

Those words saved me.

THE CHOKE

The cops eventually arrived when I was back at my mother's place in one of her spare rooms. Their bulky frames filled up the doorway. I didn't even bother getting up from the bed. They told me Lara was going to file for an apprehended violence order and they were considering charging me with trespass for jumping over the fence.

'When you find out your wife's fucking another man, let me know how you go,' I shot back at one of the constables.

I don't think they knew how to respond. They walked out without saying another word.

Lara never filed for an AVO. And I was never charged with anything, though it only occurred to me afterwards that I'd been assaulted. Conceivably I could have filed my own charges. But I left it. I didn't want to aggravate what was a bad set of circumstances for everybody, especially Evie, who'd already been through and seen too much.

I was dumb enough to still think there was hope.

* * *

It would emerge that David was a muso from Newcastle. Lara had made up the name Tim because she'd panicked. She assured me she'd not cheated on me, that she'd kissed David while we were still together but only when she knew it was over between us. In the small and incestuous live-music scene of Sydney, the couple had been introduced months before by a mutual friend of ours, a singer-songwriter called Agnes, who was now living in Portland, Oregon. I'd known her since high school.

I emailed Agnes asking for advice on how to get Lara back.

'I've been thinking of you and hoping you were okay,' she replied. 'I know there's not much you can do but ride it through. All you can really do is look after yourself. Do whatever it takes to mend your soul.'

Mend your soul.

Her trite advice was laughable. But eventually I would accept that she was right. What else was there for me to do?

I would cross paths with David again a few weeks later when through pure chance I pulled up at a red signal at a set of traffic lights, looked over at the car in the next lane and saw him staring straight back at me.

I got a good look at him this time. He was nothing special. I held his gaze but he looked down and began fiddling with the knobs on the dash radio. The cunt.

The lights changed to green and we took off in different directions. He to the west. Me to the east. I never saw him again.

* * *

So some 'soul mending' was in order. The problem for me was I couldn't just take off and 'find myself'. I was 34 years old. I had responsibilities. I was a father to a small child who needed me. I was writing five days a week for SBS and couldn't survive without the money from that job and my overseas commissions. I had no savings. The house my wife and I had bought together in the Blue Mountains west of Sydney, a rambling two-bedroom weatherboard with a beautiful garden we'd planted and watched grow together while sipping tea on our balcony, had yet to be put on the market.

I was not a spiritual person. I abhorred religion and any kind of 'alternative' therapy. I was sick of medication. I had lost interest in music and movies. I no longer had the heart for books, having watched my marriage disintegrate while writing my first one. My options for soul mending were limited. So, like many broken men do, I chose to join a dating site.

I hadn't even owned a computer when I'd got married and had only ever heard of online dating through a friend from school who had tried it and had a few salacious experiences he liked to recount over beers. I checked out the available options on the net, was amazed at how many single attractive women were on there, and put up a photo of my newly cleanshaven but horribly jowly face taken with my MacBook. Seeing myself on the screen took me aback. I was so drained of life and colour by everything that had happened it was like I'd aged 20 years. I looked faintly like Michael Douglas. And it wasn't the young, handsome version.

Online none of that mattered. Within hours I was making love to someone other than my wife for the first time in a decade: Maria, a fitness instructor with a bony frame and enormous fake breasts. We had absolutely nothing in common besides an unspoken but urgent need to be with somebody. It wasn't in any way soul mending, it wasn't even validating or particularly pleasurable – I was yearning for Lara – but it was a novelty and a distraction.

After three or four weeks of fucking between her gym classes and crying myself to sleep when I got home, I broke it off. She wanted a relationship. And I was nowhere near ready for that with her or anyone. So I made my excuses and simply found other women with whom to go through the same heartless process of introduction, seduction and abandonment.

The misery of it all hit me one night while I was fucking Carly, a girl with a dragon tattoo. A graphic designer and the mother of two kids, she'd told me, flirtingly, before we met: 'It's rather large – though not obvious – and *very* tasteful.' It was large but it was obvious and not at all tasteful: a crude red dragon that covered the small of her back to her booty dimples. The most sensuous part of a woman's body. And she'd ruined it. It wasn't sexy. It was scary.

On her bed in some McMansion suburb in the outer hills of Sydney, on my knees, ramming her from behind and trying to find enough desire to blow my load, I was being eyeballed by a badly inked serpent.

This wasn't my wife. This wasn't my life. I was in the wrong fucking movie. But I wasn't dead, either. And, for all I had just been through, that was something.

CHAPTER 3

A DRESSING SHED WITH A COFFEE DECK

TRACK 3 'Tie You Up (The Pain of Love)', The Rolling Stones, *Undercover* (1983)

There's a line in the film *When Harry Met Sally* when Meg Ryan is having one of her frequent jousts with Billy Crystal and she tells him, crankily, 'I will make love to somebody when it is making love. Not the way you do it. Like you're out for revenge or something.'

That was me. I was Harry Burns. An emasculated misery guts out for revenge on the woman who'd left him. But I was in even worse shape than Harry: I wanted to burn through as many women as possible not just to get back at Lara but also to escape from the two-headed hydra of the emptiness stemming from the separation and, worse, my by-now almost full-blown OCD. Had it morphed into sex addiction? It was never diagnosed.

Because of the nature of my illness – haunting obsessions without the usual outwardly obvious compulsions, such as hand washing, checking or counting – I had long been involuntarily assailed with the most horrible thoughts and at times was so wracked with guilt and anxiety that I felt incapable of doing work or seeing friends. The stress of the separation aggravated the symptoms a hundredfold.

The wickedness of OCD is to prey on you when you have feelings for someone – parental love, romantic love – or to latch onto the things you subconsciously fear or find most abhorrent (murder, molestation, rape, etc) and to invoke scenarios in your mind, completely involuntary on your part, that are the most disturbing and inappropriate of all. Thoughts, images, words or impulses that make you physically retch and then torture you with excruciating guilt and never-ending rumination, even though you have no control over what you think or when the thoughts, images, words or impulses come.

But where psychopaths or perverts derive pleasure from such thoughts and 'normal' people might just shrug, say, 'Christ, what was *that*?', think no more about it and get on with their lives, the person afflicted with OCD takes emotional responsibility for them. And unlike the psychopath or pervert but like 'normal' people they'll never act on their obsessions. They're frightened by them. Mortified. Utterly terrified by the unwanted thoughts their minds are producing without permission.

The person with OCD deduces that in having the thoughts something must be seriously wrong. Not with their brains but actually with *them*. So what exactly? They're 'normal' too. They have jobs. They love their families. They wish no harm on anyone and take no pleasure from the obsessions. Yet if they're having the thoughts does that mean they like what they're thinking but just don't know it?

And so a vicious cycle begins.

The heartache begets the loneliness begets the depression begets the anxiety begets the obsessions and back to the beginning to start all over again. That's the way OCD works: it preys on what you love most, when you least want it and when you're least able to fight it off. Anyone who jokes they're 'a little OCD' about tidying their house or carport just doesn't get it at all. It's not about fastidiousness or eccentricity. OCD rituals – or compulsions – take a hold on a sufferer because all they're trying to do is find a way to escape these jarring, upsetting, totally repugnant thoughts. OCD is a disorder that, coupled with depression, can drive people to suicide. For some, ending it all is a better option than admitting to anyone what you're thinking. I was close to that point myself many times.

So how I dated or fucked anyone at all after Lara walked out on me was a minor miracle. But at the time I had an overriding motivation.

My *modus operandi* was to make her jealous. I wanted her to see me with other women more desirable than her. It was the only way I thought I'd be able to get her attention. My rapidly dropping weight had made no difference. Nor had the new George Hamilton tan I was sporting courtesy of thrice-weekly sessions on a sunbed. Nor had the long letters I'd composed to plead for a second chance. Nor had the cognitive behaviour therapy or exposure and response prevention (a technique that involves confronting the thoughts head-on) I was having for the OCD. Nor had the regular counselling for the break-up, which made me realise the way I'd chosen to communicate my grief to Lara – with anger and demands for an apology – was only pushing her further away.

My 'projecting' (as she called it) served merely to confirm in her mind that her original decision to leave had been right. I'd long had a temper and became another person in moments of conflict. She wasn't going to come around to my view now, especially when she was happy with David and when it was obvious from the text messages I sent her and the tone in my voice in the rare times we spoke on the phone that I was in no headspace for temperate discussion or acknowledging my own role in our break-up. Lara agreed to one counselling session after our separation but only on the understanding it was to help me accept it was all over, not to work toward a reconciliation.

The girls I was meeting online could sense the desperation in me. I bored dates witless talking about my wife and, far from being gentlemanlike, invariably tried to sleep with them not long after delivering my woebegone spiel. Mostly I got a turned cheek but sometimes a receptive kiss, a blowjob or a fuck. Perhaps it was their way of getting me to shut up about Lara. I was surprised at how easy it was.

I never saw myself as a sex addict. What I was addicted to was the rush I got from being desired, the thrill of graduating from introductory emails or pick-up lines to getting a wink in a text or a tongue in my ear and knowing that virtually whatever I did next I was 'in', metaphorically and literally. My self-confidence, destroyed by my wife's leaving, was restored each and every time I logged on to my laptop. Sex itself was a diversion. Nothing more than a means of trying to escape a misery that shadowed my every move like a faithful but unloved dog. But it was a diversion that I came to enjoy, even relish, and for a time I had no regrets.

A DRESSING SHED WITH A COFFEE DECK

It was not just reassuring but revelatory how much these girls wanted me, a guy who had just been royally dumped, his heart torn out by his wife and his glasses smashed by a grey-haired, ponytailed guitarist with a leather jacket. They loved the words I wrote. They loved my story. They loved my jaw. They loved my stubble. They loved the fact that at a certain angle I looked like Robert Downey Jr. On one occasion, taking a ticket at a supermarket deli, the girl behind the counter stopped dead and dropped the smallgood she was holding when she saw me.

'My god. It's *you*!'

Another time, I was tapped on the shoulder by a nice young guy in a café, asking if I was the Hollywood star. I disappointed him but he still insisted on getting a photograph of his Filipina girlfriend standing next to me 'to show her family back home'.

It was all a balm to my battered ego. When I met these girls in a bar, café or restaurant I had no problems talking with them. My mother had taught me well, very early on, when I was just a teenager, to ask *questions* of women. I was a good listener. Empathetic. And appealing enough that invariably after a couple of drinks and some deep conversation we found it easy to establish a sufficient mental and physical connection to want to go to bed together. I never thought about how my behaviour would affect them. I was too deeply gripped by my own grief.

Picking up women became the most effective form of therapy I'd ever had, or at least that's how I felt about it at the time. Watching a girl's nipples harden and breasts heave as her body rose and fell from the tremors of an orgasm produced from my tongue or penis was something so desirous and perfect and gave me such complete contentment that art, literature, food, soccer, fashion, wine, rock music, all the other temporal pleasures of my small world, seemed totally inadequate in comparison. I wanted nothing more.

Over the next few years, dating became my life support. I didn't really care if I blew half a week's rent on a couple of bottles of expensive wine to help me seduce a girl, or that the small amount of money I had was in danger of disappearing. I didn't stop to consider the trail of emotional destruction I might be leaving in my wake. I was living for the moment. Drawing something at least meaningful, if not entirely tangible, from each day I was alive and putting away some experiences that were all part of the elaborate jigsaw of rebuilding my broken life.

But I was kidding myself. I couldn't let go of Lara.

* * *

I was chatting one day with a lawyer friend about the miserliness of a famous Sydney property billionaire who'd wanted me to edit his memoirs. I'd worked on a book with Australia's then richest man, the shopping-centre magnate Frank Lowy, and been recommended to the property billionaire. The old man lived in a grand apartment by the harbour but would drink cheap Queen Adelaide wine and eat frozen dinners. That's what he'd served me when I'd gone to his place for a meal. He'd died not long after.

'Hearses don't come with roof racks,' my friend had quipped.

The words had a real impact on me. What was the point of working your tail off in some stultifying office job and putting away your savings if you didn't take the time to enjoy the sun when it was out? To sit with your father at a café on weekday mornings and actually get to know him and not forever regret you missed the chance when he'd passed away? To realise the full potential of your body? To be in the position of sleeping with a beautiful woman who didn't want you for the car you drove or the house you owned or the coke you snorted off an upturned bathroom mirror but wanted you because you considered yourself to be the rarest thing of all: self-realised? I wasn't of course. Not then anyway. But I'd fooled myself into thinking I was.

Property values, interest rates, frequent-flyer points, credit lines, stock portfolios, tax offsets and all the other unbelievably unimportant shit that people spend so much of their lives worrying about didn't matter to me at all. What I told myself I was seeing with my newly single man's eyes was a world where the meaning of 'wealth' had been totally perverted. People appeared to be borrowing more than ever before and leveraging everything they had to own expensive homes and drive new cars and eat out at the right restaurants but still seemed to be fucking miserable. I cared only about *feeling* something. Emotionally I was deadened by Lara's leaving and sex awakened me not just inside but also to how I had got my priorities all wrong.

Everything that had previously preoccupied or diverted me – my career, having money for a rainy day, owning my own home – ceased to be important. I made a conscious decision that I would exist only for myself and, for half the week, my daughter. And that meant getting back my health. Enjoying simple pleasures. Learning to go without luxuries. And amid all the relentless spading and fucking, coming to understand what it was I really wanted in a woman.

* * *

After all my initial misgivings about the east, Darlinghurst struck me as just about the best place in Sydney a single man could live. A short walk from the centre of the city, in the 1920s and '30s it had been a dangerous slum where villains armed with razors ruled the streets. When I arrived with my scant possessions loaded up in a trailer it was just another gentrified suburb where bearded gay men in bad shorts had snapped up all the real estate and brought with them pricey boutiques selling more bad shorts. But it had retained a patina of its old grit and exuded an edginess that was hard to find elsewhere in Sydney, helped, in no small part, by the nightclubs, cafés, restaurants, drinking holes, medical centres, emergency rooms, shooting galleries, strip clubs and brothels that had thousands of people struggling day and night to find parking around its narrow and tightly held streets.

Its proximity to Kings Cross, Sydney's red-light district – with its methadone clinics, lively drug trade and the halfway house of the Wayside Chapel – the nearby Housing Commission-lined streets of Woolloomooloo and the sprawling St Vincent's Hospital meant there was never any shortage of junkies, transvestites, salty hookers and highly damaged people ambling up and down the main arteries of Victoria Street or Darlinghurst Road at any time of the day or night. People like the 'The Ship', a grotesquely obese man in his 50s with a Conan the Barbarian haircut who'd once been a general practitioner but had parboiled his brain drinking methylated spirits. He wore shirts that were far too small for him, exposing his distended gut to the elements. When he walked down Victoria Street in his bare feet, his pants held up with rope, he moved so slowly people inside the cafés would holler, 'The Ship is *passing*! The Ship is *passing*!'

But there wasn't a moment when I felt threatened or intimidated.

In fact I thought Darlinghurst was the perfect place to raise Evie. I wanted her to see a side of life that I believed she was being sheltered from by her mother. To go for long walks with me and photograph the beauty that existed in the palimpsest of a defaced wall, neon slicks on wet streets or paint-splattered footpaths. To get to know neighbourhood figures like Boyd, a busker with a row of missing teeth who played a guitar beautifully even with the back smashed out of it (he'd been bashed and robbed late one night by a drunken lout), and understand that they, like Daddy, were going through their own hard times but had it a lot tougher than we did.

Boyd had turned to grog and hard drugs when he'd walked in on his wife with another man. He'd gotten into some trouble with the law, watched everything he owned get taken away from him, lost contact with his kids, then spent the rest of his life on the edges trying to find some stability and purpose.

'If it hadn't been for this,' he'd told me, gesturing to his guitar, 'I don't know what I would have done. I remember not eating for a week. Just crying my eyes out. I had a hot molten ball in the pit of my stomach. The most incredible pain.'

It was never far from my mind that, had a few other things not gone my way, Boyd could have been me.

I wasn't the perfect parent. I hated watching kids' films. I went to play centres under great sufferance. I thought babycinos were solid meals. I couldn't do plaits. I said 'fuck' a lot when I was driving or cooking dinner. I sometimes zoned out when Evie needed my attention. And I allowed myself to cry in front of her when I remembered what I'd had with Lara. Sometimes those feelings of loss would overwhelm me.

But I felt I was doing the best I could do.

Many of the OCD thoughts that were torturing me so severely at that time were about my daughter. Many times I talked to her having to look away or even close my eyes because just seeing her face could spark an intrusive image, word or scenario. My main coping mechanism was to detach from her as much as I could, even though I wanted nothing more than to be close. Coupled with the depression I was already struggling with and my malignant heartache, I was spending a lot of my time not just in the purgatory of enforced loneliness but in considerable pain.

Not being able to look at the one person who loves you has to be the cruellest fate ever devised.

LAID BARE

* * *

I had come to Darlinghurst wanting to get away from everyone but, as is often the way when you're not looking for anything, found friendship and fraternity. The undisputed social hub of Victoria Street was a six-metre stretch where two long-established cafés, Nectar's Hat and Piazzolla, spilled out on to the footpath, Piazzolla with its distinctive wooden stools, aluminium tables and constant turnover of young tanned Italian and South American waitresses. These cafés were full from dawn till dusk with Sydney's richest assortment of people: bankers, tradesmen, writers, dancers, models, prostitutes, air kissers, wannabes, celebrities, lawyers, QCs, ministers, athletes, entrepreneurs, arraigned criminals, accused murderers, undercover cops, drug dealers, standover men, paparazzi photographers and the 'King of the Cross' himself, John Ibrahim, with his retinue of bodyguards. All being constantly badgered for money by the resident population of panhandlers.

In the afternoons, when the sun crested over the Horizon residential building to the west, it was like a part of Barcelona or Rome. Locals came out for *passeggiata*, to sit in the sun, meet friends, talk about sport or relationships and just watch the world go by. I was advised I had to make a choice between the two establishments. It was the done

A DRESSING SHED WITH A COFFEE DECK

thing to pick one and stick with it. The coffee was reputedly better at Piazzolla, the guys who worked there appeared to be cooler in their designer jeans and immaculate sneakers and, as far as I could tell, they seemed to have their priorities right: they spent more time looking at pretty women and talking shit with their mates than they did manning the La San Marco three-group espresso machine. It was like Bada Bing without the guns and strippers. To all appearances they had 'the life'.

Every day for about a week I sat at one of the café's folding metal banquettes, typing for an hour on my laptop. Eventually Giancarlo, the eldest of the two Calabrian brothers who worked there, asked me what I did.

'I'm a writer.'

'About what?'

'Soccer.'

'You're kidding me, right?'

'No, I write for SBS. I do a column called "Half-Time Orange".'

'*You're* HTO? I'm the biggest soccer fan there is!'

He pumped my hand for about a minute.

The next day I brought him a copy of *15 Days in June* and signed it. Giancarlo said he had a huge collection of soccer books, in Italian and English, and was always looking to add to his library. He was genuinely appreciative and it touched me. As the weeks and months went by I would bring him more books, even donate unwanted soccer shirts from my wardrobe or buy him new ones on my travels, and in return he would sidle up to my table with a snippet of gossip he had overheard from a well-placed insider or smack down the front page of *Corriere della Sera* and translate whatever was being said about the latest scandal in Serie A, the Italian league.

Raúl, the Spanish superstar from Real Madrid, had visited Piazzolla with his glamazon wife. As had Italian striker Christian Vieri, AC Milan's Daniele Massaro and Brazilian World Cup star Juninho. I would regularly arrange to lunch at the café with Pim Verbeek, the Dutch coach who took Australia to the 2010 World Cup in South Africa. Pim, a wonderful man who adored Evie and missed his own children back in the Netherlands, would later organise for Giancarlo and his son's entire soccer team to watch the Socceroos train in an otherwise closed stadium.

Players, coaches, agents, officials, journalists, political brass: there wasn't anyone inside soccer who didn't come to the café Giancarlo ran with his taciturn, dark-eyed younger brother Enrico and an oddball partner of theirs from Enrico's schooldays, Ugo, whose nose was so big and manner so prickly he was known to many around the neighbourhood as the 'Bedouin Horse Thief'.

A DRESSING SHED WITH A COFFEE DECK

I met them all there and gained their friendship and confidence.

That was the kind of place Piazzolla was: a dressing shed with a coffee deck – all in a tiny, tiled space of 33 square metres. I would always find time to go there at least once a day out of habit. And somehow, despite all the gloom that swirled around me like a black fog and the fact I couldn't play soccer to save myself, I managed to fit in. About as comfortably as Frasier Crane in *Cheers*, but I was accepted.

It was also, depressingly, beyond internet fucks and Facebook pokes, about the only social outlet I had. One of the things many people don't realise about newly separated men, especially separated fathers, is that finding opportunities to 'make time' for our friends can be extremely difficult. Friends have their own marriages and families, their own careers, and their own unique set of problems and responsibilities. Being around other people's wives and kids is not something that many separated men really want either. It's too excruciating; it only accentuates the void we feel not having ours.

Birthdays, anniversaries, Easter and Christmas are particularly emotionally taxing. So typically separated men retreat into a sort of aggravated form of loneliness, where social privations don't necessarily have to be so hard but our emotions are so jumbled and our outlook is so chronically dim that it's just easier to be completely on our own. This loneliness can become habitual and entrenched. It's also unhealthy. About as unhealthy as the studio apartments we rent. That was why the routine of going to Piazzolla each day and seeing Giancarlo and Enrico and enjoying their company, even though it was a relationship that inescapably involved the exchange of goods for money, was so important to me. The brothers were familiar enough to know who I was and ask about Evie and my work, to make me feel like I wasn't all alone and to introduce me to their families, but not familiar enough to press me on things that I wasn't ready to share with anyone.

* * *

This didn't last long, of course. When Lara met me at Piazzolla one day to do the weekly handover with Evie, and Giancarlo saw her face and how I reacted to her presence, he understood *everything*. If there was one thing Giancarlo knew more about than soccer, it was women.

At the time, he was in a relationship with an Alitalia flight attendant, 15 years his junior. Giancarlo was 45 but with his Mediterranean diet and good skin passed for 40. Classically manly in that dark Italian way with thick black hair and a dusting of grey, what he liked to call 'The Clooney',

Giancarlo estimated he'd slept with about 300 women and that number 'didn't include blowjobs'. He too had been in a marriage that had resulted in a child. He'd packed up his things in the western suburbs and come east, leaving his old life behind. But Giancarlo had felt liberated when he'd left his wife. As he told it, they'd never clicked. There was no need for him to look back. Yet I was looking back constantly. I couldn't move forward.

His bright solution was to pair me off with a Spanish girl, Agata, who was renting an apartment from him. Naturally, they'd been to bed together. One day she turned up at the café and we were introduced without me knowing anything about her. She was slim and young. Not beautiful but attractive. She worked for a liquor company, mentioned she was looking for a 'nice guy' and hated the idea of dating. She'd met too many losers. Her English wasn't great, which made conversation laborious, but we exchanged numbers and made a tentative plan to meet again.

There was clearly no future with Agata and she wasn't in any way my type. My only motive with her would be fucking, the only thing I'd been doing since the separation. But I was conflicted about the idea of taking her out on a date, talking for hours and going through the motions when she was a sweet person in an unfamiliar country who deserved her 'nice guy'. I wasn't him or ever going to be him.

I was spiritually desiccated and emotionally all over the shop. Not ready for anything so decent.

I decided not to call her. When she sent me a text about a week later, I lied and told her I was run off my feet with work. We added each other as friends on Facebook, I made a point of making a few nice comments about her holiday photos to make her feel like I wasn't ignoring her completely and the months passed without any communication. Then one Sunday, out of the blue, she sent me a text and asked what I was doing. I told her the truth: nothing. The messages went back and forth. Polite. Perfunctory. It was all going nowhere. We weren't real friends. We weren't going to be lovers. What the fuck were we?

Like so many people in this age of instant connectivity but disconnected relationships, we were occupying a sort of dead zone between being strangers and being something more yet not really having the desire to go one way or the other. Stuck in a groove of emotional embolalia. Two souls transected by boredom and randomness, clinging on to the idea that something profound and true was around the corner. But we both knew it wasn't.

I told her I could be at her place in ten minutes.

Agata asked me to fuck her in the arse like it was the most normal thing in the world. I pressed her naked body against the mirror doors of the built-in wardrobe, her

A DRESSING SHED WITH A COFFEE DECK

tanned breasts swelling on the glass, and entered her slowly. I could see postcards of her hometown in Andalucia on the wall behind me. Photos of her and her friends from happier times. Birthday cards. Her room was virtually bare. And here she was, thousands of kilometres from home, in a small room in a not very nice part of town, having one of her landlord's shadiest customers do something to her that should have been reserved for someone special and actually meant something. It struck me as desperately sad. I thought perhaps Agata just wanted me to like her; that offering anal sex was just how young people rolled these days. I certainly wasn't owed the privilege. But I was going to take it.

Days later I walked into Piazzolla.

'I just got off the phone to Agata,' Giancarlo said, smiling. 'I hate to break it to you. Mine's bigger.'

CHAPTER 4

EATING OUT

TRACK 4 'Sting Me', The Black Crowes, *The Southern Harmony and Musical Companion* (1992)

Just when it was that I went from husband to player, I cannot say. The transition was not deliberate but it was pronounced. From being a devoted family man and father, in a few short months I had reprogrammed myself to become a pantsman, a cad.

I still loved my wife and wanted to be with her more than anything else. I was a romantic: I actually still believed, as I always had, that Lara was The One. It was, obviously, why we'd married so young and had a child together. But my pleas to her were disappearing into a Grand Canyon of unanswered emails, while online, where as a friend-shy single father with equal custody and a head full of OCD I was spending the majority of my time, there were hundreds of perfectly desirable women who paid me attention, who were prepared to listen to my story, stroke my ego, hold me, spoon me, and do all the things Lara would not.

Fortuitously the ones I met seemed to be as fucked up as I was, had by their own account given up searching for their mythical Fitzwilliam Darcy and, short of full-blown intercourse, just wanted to hang out for a while IM-ing and be told before they went to sleep that they were beautiful and tomorrow was another day. It was all so mutually convenient if utterly barren.

The banality of these internet- and alcohol-facilitated encounters had their attendant pangs of despair and every now and then I pined for what I'd had before, crying in bed late at night texting my ex-wife and abusing her for the life she had denied me and my child by leaving me. Over time these feelings dimmed, as did memories of the decade of my life I'd spent with her. Only in my dreams did the silent, grainy, washed-out home movies of my marriage play out.

Emotionally I was not ready to give myself over to another woman but physically I was happy to whore myself to those I found desirable who would have me and who knew how to play the game. It was one big festival of sexual bounty and I was lost in the middle of it, not knowing where to look, overwhelmed by choice, incapable of making a decision. I was chronically afflicted with what Douglas Coupland in his novel *Generation X* calls 'option paralysis'. When given so many choices, you make none.

This is the great lie of online dating, where one in five committed relationships now begin: it promises the dream of everlasting love and happiness, true deliverance from loneliness, but in actuality it often makes monsters of the sort of men coveted by women. Swamped by options, freed from effort, the idea of commitment – usually the whole point of being on a dating site in the first place – becomes anathema. Previously good men become bounders.

I was no different from any of them. Just one of the millions of unhappy men on the internet finding deliverance through sex and the false intimacy of online hook-ups. Men constantly on the hustle and happy to forego security for spontaneity. Men wanting to make something of their fading looks and ageing physiques while they still could. Men craving the adoring attention they didn't get enough of in their failed marriages or de facto relationships. Fucking your way to happiness is as good a cathartic process as any – and an intrinsically male one.

The web is an unforgiving place to find love. A woman's value is rarely judged beyond the most primitive currency: face, tits, arse, legs. Sex on the first date becomes a given.

EATING OUT

There are rarely second ones because what gullible women think is their dream guy (handsome, athletic, independent, sensitive) has already moved on to his next conquest and is actively lining up others for after that. He doesn't care that you're upset. Why should he? You're just a Facebook friend now. Another face among hundreds of strangers.

Everyone's on the make, juggling their 'potentials' and their 'probables'. And dream guy won't stop until he's found someone he wants to fuck for the rest of his life or he reaches a point where he doesn't think he will ever do any better. He doesn't want to be a prisoner like other men he knows stuck in dead marriages with partners they've 'settled on' and unable to resist mentally undressing every other woman they meet. Husbands distracting themselves from fully accepting the misery of their existence and the enormity of their mistakes with trips to the betting shop, organised sport, home renovation and internet porn.

That is the brutal truth. Why do so many women believe otherwise? Do they really think they'll find young, fit, good-looking, educated, accomplished prospective husbands via a medium that only encourages them to act like morally feckless arseholes?

* * *

Using a variety of ever-changing online personas (RockfordFiles, CaliforniaSuite, Bergerac, Beaumarchais and sundry others), I got through them all. Businesswomen. Models, plus-size and undersize. Trolley dollies. Bellydancers. Swimmers. Nurses. Fashion editors. Food editors. Ferals. Full-blown alcoholics. Recovering alcoholics. Showgirls. The estranged wives of movie stars. Girls in toilet cubicles. Girls in steamed-up cars by footy ovals. Girls with heavy periods in plaster casts. Girls who told me they were engaged only after they'd got undressed (the clothes went straight back on). Girls who'd fuck visiting celebrities and sell their stories to the gossip rags.

I'd drive up and down the coast, sometimes for six-hour round trips, to bang single mothers on kitchen benches. I'd fly interstate on an hour's notice to rendezvous in five-star hotel rooms with fake-titted 19-year-olds. I'd get chased down the street by loopy poets I'd fingered then burned off with the 'it's not you, it's me' speech. I'd administer cunnilingus to French backpackers as they swung on the rails of the bunk bed I'd erected for Evie over my own. I'd pick from my teeth the stray pubes of socialists who'd never waxed. I'd have 'Skype sex' with lonely expatriates on webcam in places as far afield as Kenya and Quebec, where both of us got naked and masturbated in front of our cams before making promises to each other we knew, deep down, we would never keep. I'd even date two girls in one night. Fuck one at 9pm. The other at 11. I lost count of the number of women I slept with. It all went by so fast. A zoetrope of female body parts. It was almost a full-time job. It *was* my job.

Who and what had I become?

In fact I performed this sleazy charade so often that I was able to decipher the code in a woman's profile and determine even before I'd met her just how easy it would be to get her in the sack and what she would do when she was in it. They are the signs every player on a dating site looks for and a lot of men know and joke about but won't ever let on because usually they are proven right.

'Spontaneous' is read as 'fucks on the first date'. 'Adventurous' as 'will do anal'. 'Separated' as 'buy condoms'. Any woman who puts all those words on a dating website with no conception of how most men will read it is asking for a heap of trouble. Players don't care if a girl is 'down to earth' or 'genuine' or she reads Eckhart Tolle. They don't fucking care. With players it's all about fuckability. Durability has nothing to do with it. Dare write 'bubbly' (short, overweight and irritating), 'conservative' (not on the first date, bud) or 'I love animals' (potential cat lady) and you can expect an empty inbox. Unless, of course, you're a swimwear model with a pretty face and an enormous rack. In which case you can write 'I kill people for fun' and it won't matter.

How Men Read Women's Online Dating Profiles

Adventurous – does anal

Anaïs Nin – fucks on the first date

Are you out there? – yes, but I'm ignoring you

Athletic – average

Average – has 'tuckshop lady arms' aka 'bingo wings'

Be the change you want to see in the world – she paid money to see *Eat, Pray, Love*

Bridget Jones – has a muffin top

Bubbly – short, overweight and irritating

Christian – she'll suck it, as long as I don't tell anyone

Conservative – not on the first date, bud

Curvy – big arse

Dance like no one is watching – dances like everyone is watching

Devoted – will never get rid of her

Don't care about looks – will fuck for money/looking for a sugar daddy

Easygoing – your mates are fair game

Fashionable – will end up spending all my money on her

Free spirited – see *Anaïs Nin*

Genuine – quite desperate

I'm attractive – no, you're not

I appreciate good design – don't even think about taking me back to your filthy dump

If you like pina coladas and getting caught in the rain – yes, she really is that boring

I love life – medicated

I'm looking for someone to complete me – far, *far* from being complete

I'm no good at writing about myself – no redeeming qualities whatsoever

I'm still working on my profile. Nudge me to update it by sending a kiss message – so hot she doesn't need to bother

Is it you I'm looking for? – no

I loved *Shantaram* – doesn't read

Live, laugh, love – depressed

Looking for my knight in shining armour – self-absorbed bitch

Looking for my prince – see above

Love animals – potential cat lady

Love to travel – see *Fashionable*

Low maintenance – Sherwood Forest

Loyal – not getting any

My family are very important to me – they will fucking hate me

My friends are very important to me – I will fucking hate them

Non-judgmental – out of rehab

Old fashioned – missionary only, and with the lights out please

Open minded – threeway

Sensuous – swallows

Separated – buy condoms

Spiritual – undefined sexual boundaries

Spontaneous – see *Anaïs Nin*

What have you got to lose? – my dignity

Where's my Darcy? – total pain in the arse

There are some women who know this code. I met one of them, Suzi, very early on. A primary-school teacher from Centennial Park going through an acrimonious live-in separation from her futures-trader husband, she invited me over one night when her kids had just gone to bed and her husband was out drinking with friends. There was no getting-to-know-you chat on the couch with a glass of New Zealand sauvignon blanc or discussion about what CD to put on. She gave me clear instructions in her email: *Don't knock on the door. Go through the side gate. Meet me out the back in the courtyard. Don't talk to me.*

I did as I was told and Suzi was waiting for me. She took off her slip dress, got on her knees on the cold paving tiles and pulled my pants down. She began by sucking my balls, stroking the shaft of my cock with one hand and sticking a finger in my arse with the other, and then started to deep throat me, hard and vigorously. Her head was slapping against my abdomen. This went on for a couple of minutes before I pulled her up, pushed her against the wall under the kitchen window and sodomised her. When I was ready to come she turned around, fell to the ground again and held my gaze while I ejaculated on her face and in her hair, Japanese *bukkake* style. It was the hottest, most animalistic sexual encounter I'd ever had. And we hadn't said a word to each other.

EATING OUT

Suzi picked up her dress, using it to wipe off the ejaculate I'd decorated on her face like icing from a piping bag, leaned forward and French-kissed me. It was time to go. I'd been there all of ten minutes. I didn't look back when I closed the side gate behind me. There was no need. These were the rules of the game.

* * *

My womanising got so crazy at one point that a higher power decided to intervene. Driving late one night to a hook-up on the northern beaches, my car exploded on Military Road in Mosman outside the apartment building of a sweet mother of two boys I'd been seeing and who wanted a relationship, but who I'd stood up that evening to take the booty call. I spent two hours waiting for a tow truck, terrified she'd come out and bust me for having lied to her. She didn't, but it was a sign I needed to slow down and grow up.

Gabrielle, a 42-year-old 'mature' model who looked so much like Lara that any thoughts of my wife were momentarily banished, offered a shot at normalcy. I had not taken things anywhere with Lara's other doppelgänger, Brooke, and perhaps that had been a mistake. She'd since moved in with the editor of a well-known porn magazine. So I'd missed my chance. I was determined not to make the same mistake twice.

As with a lot of online romances, the fact Gabrielle lived a thousand kilometres away in Melbourne, was the mother of two kids (including a two-year-old girl she was breastfeeding) and had just left a 17-year marriage with a violent, abusive man who'd dragged her kicking and screaming into a vicious legal dispute in the Family Court didn't matter a jot.

For the uninitiated, that's often the way it is with love on the net. You're so caught up in the adrenalin of meeting someone who appears to be everything you could wish for in a person and is holding out the immediate prospect of sex that you pay no heed to such crucial details. Via a blizzard of emails, text messages, picture messages, pokes, likes, IMs, winks, smileys and XXXs you're caught up in an irresistible wave of counterfeit intimacy that only peters out – and sometimes halts dramatically – when you actually physically meet. That's when reality bites.

When Gabrielle picked me up from Avalon airport outside Melbourne we kissed before we even spoke. She was trembling with nerves. We got in her expensive, brand-new SUV and started driving towards the city, some light music on the radio to break the uncomfortable silence. It was clear she was overwhelmed by the situation. After about half an hour she told me she had to stop the car. She pulled over by the side of the highway and got out, breathing heavily.

EATING OUT

She was having a panic attack. I had to stroke her hair and shoulders for her to relax.

'It's okay,' she smiled, out of breath. 'I think I'm going to be alright. I just need some air.'

After about five minutes we got back in the car and continued to her home in St Kilda, where the moment we got through the door we fucked on top of the dishwasher.

But it would get even weirder.

Later Gabrielle told me she had to go pick up her two-year-old daughter and five-year-old son from her ex, who would be meeting her in a McDonald's car park. The pick-up and drop-off arrangements were all mandated by a judge. She didn't want me in the house when they got home. Nor, because of the court case, did she want the kids reporting to their dad that there was a strange man staying with their mum. Gabrielle asked that I go to a café, leave it 20 or 30 minutes for her to collect the kids, drive home and have them settled, then walk back and knock on the door as if I were a friend just paying an impromptu visit. The kids would rush to the door and be none the wiser that this stranger from Sydney had just been boffing their mother. My bags were hidden in the locked study so they wouldn't twig I had been there.

Once inside, Gabrielle would go through the pantomime of inviting me to stay for dinner, the kids would get very excited, and they'd go to bed early, leaving me adequate time to have sex with their mother again before I'd retire and set up camp in the study. She couldn't run the risk of me being caught in her bed. Gabrielle would set the alarm and at 7am, just before the kids would rise for the day, I'd get dressed in new clothes, leave the study and walk out onto the porch, shutting the front door behind me. When the kids stirred to wake, that was my cue to knock. Gabrielle would get the kids to answer and, as we expected, they were thrilled that the funny man from the night before just happened to be walking in the area and had thought it would be a nice surprise to pop over for breakfast.

This nonsense went on for three days.

The bubble of adrenalin had well and truly burst by then. I ended it with a disappointed but exhausted Gabrielle and went back to Darlinghurst. I was happy to go home. At least the games I played there were over quickly and weren't so fucking complicated.

* * *

Kristin, an elegant, refined, 40-year-old banker way above my station (patrician bearing, Barbara Hershey lips), agreed to a date at an hour's notice late on a Saturday night. We met in Double Bay, a suburb not far from Darlinghurst but a world away in social attitudes and average income. Horrible.

EATING OUT

But I wasn't feeling fussy. I was out for sex and Kristin looked an easy touch, even though I sensed she knew I was damaged goods the moment I walked into the empty bar and ordered a cocktail.

As with all the others, I downloaded my story of woe and then made a pass at her, telling her she had 'very kissable lips' and moving in with the restraint of a Turkish rug seller. She politely accommodated me but that was as far as I was going to get that night.

'You're not ready for anyone,' she said. 'You're not over your wife.'

Sharp as well as beautiful. I went in for the kill again but Kristin would have none of it. She was quite adamant about it. She paid for the bill and left. Even when I tried jokingly tailing her turbo-diesel BMW Z4 through the back streets of Double Bay to her hilltop home in Darling Point, she managed to lose me.

Kristin called me the next day and we had some fairly unthrilling sex. And a few times after that. But soon we realised we were better at being friends. The chemistry wasn't there. There was nothing more to it than that. Our politics were wildly incompatible (she would have voted for the long-dead Sir Robert Menzies, given half a chance). Plus she had her shit together. She owned a house. Had a real career. Put away money. Everything I wasn't doing. What Kristin ever saw in me I will never know but she went on to become the best female friend I'd ever had. And it was the most unexpected gift I could have hoped for at that time in my life.

I loved women but I was threatening to become a misogynist. My new friend pulled me back to reality.

She wasn't shy with her opinions. She told me that I was a cliché, a fuckwit, that I owed it to Evie to pull myself together, that Lara's heart, despite everything, was still winnable.

She looked out for me.

'Hey Fink,' she wrote to me from work one day. 'Promise me this, please. Whatever you do, don't see *The Notebook*. It'll *kill* you.'

She went to Lara's shop and pretended to be a customer, only to return and tell me she was 'just lovely'. It wasn't what I wanted to hear. Despite loving Lara, it was so much easier to hate her.

This is one of the unexpected pleasures of online dating. It's not all tawdry. Unsuccessful dates can turn into successful friendships. Good, selfless people that you have been waiting to meet all your life suddenly appear and provide insight, comfort and support at the most critical times. You are bonded by shared experience, by the vicissitudes of love and loss. (Kristin had her own hard-luck story: cheated on by her boyfriend of eight years.) And you have the kind of ready empathy you won't always get from your family or oldest friends. Your new friends are veterans of their own romantic wars, too, with their own stories. That, in truth, was the biggest reward out of that period of my life, not all the notches on my belt.

When I was in my lows, and I had many of them from loneliness, OCD and depression, Kristin, besides my parents, was the person I turned to and always knew would be there.

She even brought me back to earth with some plain talking.

'Fink, you *have* to get fit. If a friend can't tell you, who can?'

And this was a woman so straight she owned a Rick Astley album. I might as well have been the antichrist. Were it not for our computers, the whole concept of us ever meeting was palpably absurd.

* * *

Just as it was absurd to go on feeling sorry for myself after meeting Isabella, a well-raised Italian-Australian girl from the western suburbs of Sydney who'd married the scion of a wealthy Danish family in a grand wedding in Europe. They returned to Australia and had a baby boy not long after. When the child was only three months old and just a week after his christening, Isabella came home from an Easter weekend at her parents' house to find her rich, handsome, blond, well-to-do husband in a bath full of red water and the back of his head blown out. He was still holding the gun under his chin. He'd left his diary on the kitchen bench with a note inside it that began, 'I love you, Isabella, I'm a failure' and contained the password to his computer.

Isabella hadn't even had a chance to help him. She knew nothing about his secret world of drugs, alcohol and other addictions, including women. They only became apparent when she sat down, typed in the password and read the journal he'd left on the desktop computer.

She had lost not just her marriage and her future but her son's father. I still had Evie and she had me. My daughter would grow up knowing her mother. Isabella's son would never know his father. And so long as Lara was alive, I conceivably still had a chance with her. Who knew when she would come around? Stranger things had happened.

Isabella, a beautiful, graceful woman undeserving of such a tragedy, wouldn't get any chances. Later, she would be diagnosed with breast cancer. Typically, she fought that battle with the same courage and self-effacement she had shown after the death of her husband.

'I'm sick of being my friends' benchmark for pity,' she told me over coffee at Piazzolla one day.

I was a lucky man. And I needed to lighten the fuck up.

CHAPTER 5

DIVORCED FATHERS AND DAUGHTERS ALL-STARS

TRACK 5 'Way Down Now', World Party, *Goodbye Jumbo* (1990)

Nineteen seventy-nine was UNESCO's International Year of the Child. I remember it for its exquisite irony because it was the year my parents, Sal and Alby, decided to break up.

The five of us – me, Mum, Dad, my younger sister Tammy and younger adopted brother Toshi, an orphan who'd got out of Saigon on one of the last 'Operation Babylift' rescue missions during the Vietnam War – were living the idyllic Australian coastal life in an old house on the hill at Balmoral Beach, an exclusive enclave on Sydney's lower north shore, back when it was still possible for normal people to afford to live there. Sal and Alby bought the house in 1975 for $78,000. Today it's worth about $7 million, and still hasn't been renovated.

As a six-year-old, though, I spent a good part of that year getting caned by teachers for wanting to run home and be with my mother and father to stop them breaking up. One of the few photographs I have of them together, a Polaroid, was taken right after I'd separated them during a fight. Asleep upstairs, I'd been woken after midnight by the yelling and screaming and came down to the living room in my pyjamas, dressing gown and slippers. They did their best to smile for the camera, their arms warily around each other. By taking the photo, I thought I was magically saving my family.

It was futile, of course.

My father wasn't getting what he needed physically from the marriage and had a string of discreet affairs. It was his way, he told me decades later, of not going spare while managing to stay with the woman he loved, my mother. But it got messy. After discovering his infidelity, Sal found the understanding and intimacy she hadn't got from my father with one of his friends.

While putting up a TV aerial on the roof one day, Alby had an epiphany that he wanted to save what they had and give up on the other women. But the relationship by then was totally fractured. Sal told him she needed time for herself. She went to Bali and stayed in rat-infested guesthouses. When she got back to Australia they tried to make it work, but it was over between them. She asked him to leave. Her friends, just as Lara's friends would 28 years later, encouraged her to go through with the separation.

My father ran off to Auxerre in France with a side trip to the Far East and worked on a barge, later hiding away in the Balearic Islands of Spain, writing me postcards and letters, asking after Sal. 'Hope soccer and cubs are OK,' he wrote on one postcard from Japan. 'Love to Mummy. Your bud, Dad.' He even wrote a 24-page book of poems that he self-published and dedicated to my mother. A little book of verse spilling over with sadness, homesickness and yearning. It wouldn't break her resolve, even when out of sheer desperation he got me to ask her to come back. She got the divorce. A couple of years later my father met an attractive younger woman, Penny, and they married.

My mother, by contrast, would largely give up on men. In her 40s she fell in love with a nudist carpenter from Nimbin (he'd been introduced to me in my early teens wearing nothing but a nail bag), had a third son and went on to have her heart broken again when the nudist ended the relationship. She was 59 when I split from Lara. My father was 61 and still married to Penny.

By now you'd think Sal and Alby might have buried the hatchet, kicking back together on a garden seat on a summer afternoon, long drinks in hand, reminiscing about the good times before their own rupture and watching their grandkids gambol about on the lawn like bear cubs in a summer meadow. But they still act like it's 1979. At important family functions, such as my wedding, they can at least tolerate each other's presence. Birthdays and Christmas, however, remain strictly segregated affairs.

I'd been putting up with this cold war for longer than I cared to remember and without doubt it had dramatically affected my personality, my own view of relationships and the loyalty I felt to both parents. I tend to take Dad's side in arguments. My sister, Tammy, usually takes Mum's. For a long time Sal was upset with Alby for making me feel responsible for the divorce. In return Alby was upset with Sal for not wanting him back, even though with Penny he is now happier than he's ever been.

We are a divided family.

I never wanted this kind of thing to happen to Lara and me. Which was why I'd only married her totally convinced that I could never want another woman and we'd never break up. At our wedding, a picnic for friends and family in the beautiful grounds of an art college with a string quartet playing Led Zeppelin, we'd even stood before a reverend of the Uniting Church, Dr David Millikan, and listened to a long but utterly compelling speech about the true test of marriage being how you get through those times when you can barely stand to look at each other. It blew a lot of people away. Far from pissing on our parade, the good reverend was actually giving us a lecture on what he saw as the true meaning of love. Love wasn't just about happiness, passion and companionship, it was about trial and perseverance.

Yet all around me, at every bar I propped my elbows on, in every row of seats I sat on at the soccer, on every beach I jogged up and down trying to pass the minutes, hours and days when I was without Evie as a divorced father, I'd come across lost and lonely men just like me who'd had similar hopes of the permanence of love and made the decision to get married but were now picking up the pieces of their shattered lives, wondering how they could have got it so wrong.

They were easy to recognise. The guy with the laptop in the crowded pub. The guy eating Japanese alone. The guy with the paunch and the dreadful gait trying to get fit in the park. The guy lifting weights that were far too big for him in the gym. The guy with the son wearing school shoes on a weekend because his ex had forgotten to send over in his schoolbag the pair of new sneakers he'd bought him to wear. I met one poor sap late on a summer's afternoon on Tamarama Beach who confided while our two daughters played in the surf that he'd just gone to his ex-wife's wedding. She'd left him barely three months before, married a man as old as her father and now lived in a mansion in Bellevue Hill. He was living in a rented room just up the road. He said he was happy for her but I could sense he was just trying to put on a brave front. I wanted to hug him. Instead we just stood there, as so many men do in these situations, folding our arms and keeping a safe distance, united by wretchedness while watching the last light of a Sydney summer's day evaporate over the Tasman Sea.

* * *

Why is there this epidemic of heartbreak when finding true love is supposed to be easier than ever because of technology? Simply because getting out of relationships is also easier than ever because of technology.

The online world and the ease with which it facilitates hook-ups between people who would otherwise never have met in 'real life' means the rules of relationships have changed. The rules of dating have changed. Women have become more like men. Men, already by their very nature incorrigible sexual opportunists, have become worse. Few men can really be bothered with old-fashioned courting when it's so easy to fuck a different girl every night of the week. And not just in their suburb or city, but around the country, around the world.

Emails and text messages allow liaisons to be more secretive. Online dating, chat rooms, social-networking sites and apps such as Badoo encourage curiosity, flirtation and infidelity. The web has become one vast treasure hunt for the perfect mate.

Twenty years ago taking a picture of an erect cock or naked breasts and getting it delivered to the desired recipient took some doing. Now it can be done in seconds. Instantly. To anywhere on the planet. Internet porn and raunch culture have upended ideas about what is considered standard in the bedroom and set higher benchmarks for sexual performance and physical appearance. So many couples exist in a state of perpetual anxiety. Is the life they have made together actually good enough? Is their partner someone they really want to fuck for the rest of their lives? Can they do better? In this new connected world, sure they can. Or at least they're fooling themselves into thinking they can.

We're living in the age of distraction, where inexhaustible options haven't delivered us serenity. Rather discontent. Dissatisfaction. In the United Kingdom, Facebook alone is cited as a cause in one in three divorces. In the United States, it's been put as high as one in five, though with some dispute as to the veracity of the figure. Whatever the case, technology is having a massive impact on traditional relationships. They've effectively suffered the fate of porn movies: been reduced to 'scenes', designed for short attention spans and instant gratification rather than rewarding patience.

The internet and smartphones have had as catastrophic an impact on modern love in the 2000s as refined sugar did on waistlines in the 1900s. There are more Apple products in American homes than there are married couples. We're only now starting to wake up to the genie we've unleashed but it's not something that can be put back in the bottle. It's out there. In many cases destroying lives, not improving them.

My relative popularity online, courtesy of my ability to write coherent sentences, decent looks and a rapidly thinning face, meant I could take my pick of virtually anyone I liked, vetting candidates on the most superficial of attributes. Too often for me the endgame was fucking, not the happily ever after, so that meant big tits, small waists, gamine faces, lissome bodies. Women who had 'tuckshop lady arms' or 'wizard sleeves' didn't get a look-in. I was a bastard because I could be. It was all so mercenary but all so ridiculously easy. I assured myself I wasn't doing anything that anyone else wasn't doing. And, having lost my moral scruples, I saw no reason to stop unless someone amazing came along. I had one life. And Lara, in the throes of passion with her new man, wasn't about to have some road-to-Damascus moment and come back to me. As Alby would often say, and he knew this as well as anyone from all those nights howling at the moon on the deck of a barge in Burgundy: 'Life's a marathon, son. Not a short-course sprint race.'

* * *

Ron didn't look like he could do any short-course sprint racing. He wasn't up for much movement at all. A big unit in his early 40s with close-cropped greying hair and a couple of chins, standing well over six foot and packing 120 kilograms under his company-monogrammed polo shirt, he spent his working week driving his big Ford sedan from Sydney to the dusty far west of New South Wales and back again, visiting clients of his financial-planning business and spending far too much time in McDonald's drive-thrus.

We had been introduced through mutual friends and Ron had become my financial adviser. Seeing as I'd taken to searching for coins in the folds of my sofa, it wasn't an especially lucrative arrangement for him, but he knew a bit about soccer, was a father to two young girls around Evie's age and, as I was to discover the first time we met for coffee, was going through a terrible divorce of his own, a real *War of the Roses* donnybrook, with serried ranks of lawyers and child psychologists. It was all very fresh.

On returning home from one of his trips out west, he'd pulled into the driveway of his house in Cronulla and heard noises coming from inside. When he parted a bush and put his nose to the window he was greeted by the sight of his naked wife of 15 years entangled with a complete stranger, also naked, on the living-room floor. But when Ron tapped the window, they didn't stop. Being a gentle, sensitive soul not given to confrontation, he returned to his car and sat in the driver's seat while the pair continued fucking. He waited a few minutes then went back.

'Is it over?' he asked his wife through the deadlocked front door.

'What do you *fuckin'* reckon?' she shot back. 'Now leave me *alone* so I can keep fucking this *guy*!'

Her 'guy' turned out to be a serving officer of the New South Wales police. When the coppers weren't attending to domestic disputes like mine with Lara they were right in the middle of them, pants down, cocks out, inside other men's wives.

Like me, Ron pitched up at his mum's. But he was smart enough to go straight to his lawyer. He didn't end up unconscious in a garden bed with his glasses smashed and potting soil in his mouth. He was now in court, embroiled in a bitter custody dispute which was further complicated by the delicate matter of extricating his wife from his business (she was a part owner) and fending off an AVO application she had made through her cop lover.

Having her removed from the family company, gaining equal access to his kids and putting the AVO to bed would end up costing Ron hundreds of thousands of dollars. But he was resolute in not giving her any more than she deserved.

Just as I was resolute in making sure he didn't make the same mistakes I had early on in my separation, slide into a pit of depression and despair and attempt to go back to the woman who'd been so cruel to him. When he was at his lowest there wasn't a day when I didn't ring Ron to make sure he wasn't going to do something stupid. Frequently when I got him on the phone he'd just gibber like an idiot. His decision-making was totally shot. Rubbing one out was vitally important.

'Mate, wank as much as humanly possible – wank five times a day if you have to,' I urged him, just as I had to get through the loneliest times when I physically ached for Lara. '*FLOG* yourself.'

Ron was doing it particularly tough, having to go through a solicitor to schedule mediation for the most basic parenting decisions, such as school pick-ups and drop-offs – even what bed he chose for his kids to sleep in on their scheduled visits. As much as my own wife had been awful to me, at least I could talk to Lara about such things without acrimony.

To lighten Ron's emotional load I suggested our abbreviated families regularly meet for dinner at Itami, a

Japanese restaurant on Darlinghurst Road. The truth, though, was that I also needed the company. We called it the Divorced Fathers and Daughters All-Stars, a play on Woody Allen's Sunday baseball team in *Manhattan*, the Divorced Fathers and Sons All-Stars. Our girls – none older than seven – would make a terrible mess of their sushi rolls. Almost as bad as the mess Ron and I had made of our marriages.

'How have you been?' he'd start when we sat down.

'Good, mate, good.'

'Okay, but are you right … in *yourself*?'

It was a mark of his character that he asked me this question every time I saw him. Though outwardly a typically inscrutable Australian bloke, my new friend was a sensitive man.

Ron had had his own online-dating misadventures. Blowjobs with soccer mums in parked cars outside shopping centres. Come-and-run *bukkake* meets with bored housewives in the bush. Straight-up anal sex with goths. He'd even banged a famous Australian 'personality' doggy style over the armrest of a chaise longue on their first date. After the second she raised the idea of getting married. Ron cooled it off. It would prove a wise decision. She'd fall pregnant to another man a month later.

Far from being emotional islands, Ron and I were just looking for someone to tell us everything was going to be alright, even though we didn't know what the fuck we were doing ourselves. It's why we gravitated to each other and, with our daughters, became a kind of family of our own. It's why we sought out the company of women who appreciated us when the women we loved wouldn't, even if it was only for an hour in an unfamiliar bed or the back seat of a car. Being inside our own heads was like walking a wasteland of regrets.

My father, the only other man I could really confide in about my deepest problems, understood that. It was why he told me to 'stop being Hamas' with Lara and find some inner peace.

'Continuing to lob rockets just reduces everything to ruin,' he said in a letter. 'Change tack. Forgive the hurt that has been inflicted on you. Endure with grace what you can't change.'

It was why he dropped by my flat unannounced at all hours of the day, seeing if I needed anything fixed and, if I didn't, fixing things anyway. He put up bookshelves. He made me hat racks. He sorted my shirts by colour. He cleaned my toilet, a forbidding sunken cave of black terror that hadn't been touched since the Apollo moon landings.

It was also why he told me to start running. When he'd separated from my mother, that's what he'd done. Sixty kilometres a week. Day and night. Whatever the weather. No matter how bad he felt. He'd even written a short story about it, published in *Billy Blue*, a Sydney literary magazine, back in the 1980s. Then, he'd been 'a troubled man taking it out on the concrete', and now, 30 years later, so was I. Through rainstorms along the coast at dusk. Along country trails. Half marathons. Father and son. The full circle. A proud lineage of shin splints and wrecked families.

* * *

What had I done to have this cruel symmetry imposed on me? By now Lara was even accusing me of using Evie against her, much in the manner Sal had accused Alby of using me to try to save their marriage. Sal backed her up. It was, she maintained, why she'd called me a 'cunt'. It wasn't true. All I wanted was my family back. The whole. Hadn't I spent my childhood and adult life learning from the mistakes of my parents? Or had I just been destined to repeat them?

Lara and I had both come from broken homes. We'd gone out of our way to create for each other something far more solid and nurturing than the relationships of our parents.

But perhaps because of their respective failures we were being set up for disaster rather than being destined to succeed in spite of them. My mother had been right all along. I was a 'little Alby' to the laces of my running shoes.

DIVORCED FATHERS AND DAUGHTERS ALL-STARS

But at least I was finally starting to look like the man I used to be. I dropped 30kg because of running. I saw abdomen muscles I hadn't seen since I was 21. Physically I was in the best shape of my life. I'd started working out daily, for two hours straight, mostly at a community gym down in the tough waterside pocket of Woolloomooloo. There I met former ice addicts and ex-cons who'd lost everything and hit rock bottom only to turn their lives around through exercise. I had no excuses not to get fit. Mentally I was starting to tame my demons simply by feeling better about myself and having a focus outside my obsessions. Emotionally, though, I was still struggling. Hoping clarity and peace would come but sabotaging my recovery with a succession of stupid decisions and an excessive amount of self-blame.

* * *

The biggest challenge newly separated men face is filling time. Quiet moments are pregnant with terror. Nights are the worst. When no one calls. When no one is poking you. When you can't watch TV or read a book because your overtaxed mind is like a blown circuit board. So you do something physical. You lift weights. You pound the streets. Or you punch a bag. And if you can't get to a 24-hour gym, you sort black socks, whack off in front of porn, drink a bottle of whisky or crank up AC/DC's *Powerage*, the most visceral, honest insight into the psychology of damaged men available anywhere. Anything to take yourself away from that place you don't want to go: inside your head.

Naturally, you also make some unbelievable mistakes with women through sheer loneliness. I made plenty.

Such as inviting a 48-year-old stranger I'd met online to my flat to give me an erotic massage only to discover when she arrived that her derriere literally filled the width of the doorway. She was like the fat lady in the Eddie Murphy movie *Norbit*. There was no way I could get out of it. But it worked out better than I expected. With my eyes closed, she ended up giving me one of the best blowjobs of my life. So much for 'types'.

Or when I struck up an IM chat of an evening with a good-looking interior designer and proceeded to talk with her for five hours on the phone. At 3am she booked a cab and fronted up to my place in her dressing gown and night slip. When she got in my bed she froze like she'd seen a ghost.

'I want to go back to my husband,' she stammered, putting her gown back on and closing the door behind her without so much as even looking back at me.

Or when I fell for an Italian girl, again online, who was happy to email me and talk on the phone, even to my father, but every time I arranged to meet her she'd come up with an excuse not to meet. This went on for months. She stood me up a dozen times and, being totally naive, I'd keep coming back for more humiliation, even fronting up at her door only to be turned away because she was contagious or had just had dental surgery or whatever other excuse she could come up with. I convinced myself that she was just shy and was motivated to keep trying by the fact she was an exceptionally beautiful woman. At least according to her profile photo.

Or when I began a futile Skype relationship with a volunteer working in a remote panda sanctuary in Xinjiang. Futile because she was stuck in a bamboo grove in the middle of China and would be for years; I was stuck in a prison of thoughts of where I'd gone wrong with Lara. The feelings I developed for her just added to the hurt and isolation I was already experiencing.

Or when I agreed to a date with *two* women. The three of us. I thought it was going to end up in something wonderful and illicit but halfway through it dawned on me I was just being used as a bit of comic relief by two bored narcissists who were used to getting their way with gullible and desperate men. I walked out.

Or when I bareback-fucked a somewhat unhinged writer from Paddington I'd been set up with by friends and in the regulation post-coital pillow chat was breezily informed,

'Oh, *by the way*, Jesse, I just wanted you to know I have herpes, but I didn't know how to tell you!' I'd test clear.

Those lapses of judgment were relatively innocent. But I could also be wilfully stupid. There was one woman who caught me at a time when I was feeling particularly desolate, Lara having gone to court to file for divorce. This individual contacted me online, paid me compliments and made me feel so much better about myself in our subsequent IM exchange that the fact she hadn't shown me her photo seemed an irrelevance. She went on to talk dirty and I masturbated, albeit with little pleasure, to the words she was typing on the screen.

When afterwards she gave me her address in Darling Harbour and asked me to come over and fuck her for real, I asked her to oblige with a photo. She was plain and unattractive. I made up some story about having to be somewhere the next day and logged off. I felt terribly ashamed. When she tried to get in touch with me again, even sending me an email from a holiday abroad recounting her activities like we were lovers, I ignored her.

Months passed and an email landed in my inbox from a woman who said she lived in Watsons Bay. She told me she'd only just listed her profile on the dating site I was on, hadn't had time to put up a photo and what did I have to lose but to go meet her for a drink? She assured me I'd be happy. It was late on a rainy Sunday night and I had nothing else to do. So I walked into the pub not far from my flat and a girl at a corner table wearing a hat with a peak that obscured her eyes beckoned me over. I ordered a drink and we began talking. But there was something about her that seemed familiar. It bugged me. I asked her if we'd met before. She said we hadn't. I replied that I was sorry, I was sure we had. I must have mistaken her for someone else. To which she looked me coldly in the eye and said something that still chills me to this day.

'Really? And was she a *psycho*?'

I held her gaze. It was the same girl I'd brushed off; she'd just picked another name, put on a hat and dyed her hair. I was genuinely scared. I didn't even finish my beer. I got up as fast as I could and left, swearing to never again be so fucking cavalier with my and my daughter's safety.

That's what being accidentally single again does to men. It scrambles their minds. Makes them do things they would not normally contemplate. Your sex drive is like it was when you were 20 but you don't have the same social freedoms you did back then, especially when you factor in the single father's gift/single man's curse of equal custody. So you take risks. Take what you can. And more often than not find yourself going home unhappier than you were before, much lighter in the wallet and wondering whatever happened to your dignity.

Going from the social cachet of marriage and the structure of family in your mid-20s to being separated and single again in your mid-30s is like being transported from the paradise of earth to the harsh red planet of *Total Recall*. You can't so much as breathe if you leave the mental bubble of your past. You try to erase the memories of the life you used to have but feel compelled to relive them, over and over, looking for the clue that's going to solve the riddle of your pain. The gravity of it all hits you hardest when you get turned away at nightclub doors and those dinner invitations you used to get with your wife don't come anymore. They liked her. Not you. Or at least they could tolerate you *with* her. Or you walk into a bookshop and come by the 'Parenting' section. You used to spend a lot of time there. Full of hope, planning for the future. Now it's time to move a couple of feet to the right. *There.* You'll find everything you need in 'Self Help', you dismal old fuck.

CHAPTER 6

TURBULENCE ADDICTION

TRACK 6 'Fire Woman', The Cult, *Sonic Temple* (1989)

Kristin thought it was the rescuer in me. Part of my turbulence addiction. I thought it was just a predilection for beautiful, bohemian, creative women. Dark-eyed odalisques lifted straight from a Henri Matisse painting. Straight-fringed, bike-riding Jane Birkin types in Breton stripes. Crazily dressed Annie Halls. But, to my friend's credit, there was a pattern in my romantic life post Lara that was striking: a fatal attraction to what Kristin sneeringly called (as only she could) 'the psychotic and the helpless': women who needed help, medication or hospitalisation yet hit all the sexual markers I'd laid out for a prospective mate. I'd fall for three such women in a row.

I was a victim and I was ineluctably drawn to other victims, the more fucked in the head the better. These women could never give me the ballast I needed but they could give me empathy and understanding. Crucially, they could also give me the passion that had been drained from my life since the separation.

There can be something incredibly sexy in the alchemy of dysfunction, when two doomed people come together (Romeo and Juliet, Bonnie and Clyde, Harold and Maude, Thelma and Louise). And that's what I wanted more than anything. To feel the electricity of desire and being desired. Coursing through two bodies at the same time. It hadn't happened very often in my adult life so I didn't care if I got it from psychotics or the helpless or anyone addled with some diagnosable malaise. I was picky with the physical appearance of women but undiscriminating when it came to their problems.

And who the fuck was I to judge them anyway when I had a cracking disorder of my own?

* * *

Chloe was a short, gorgeous, thick-browed, olive-skinned photographer who lived in Brisbane. We found each other through a dating site and parked each other as friends on Facebook for about six months before she announced she was coming down to Sydney for an exhibition of her photographs of Tuva in eastern Russia. That she had even been to Tuva, a republic in Siberia best known for its throat singers, was a turn-on of its own. I like intrepid women. But when we met I got that electricity I desired and more. It was instant chemistry. We went back to Chloe's hotel in the city and fucked so enthusiastically and insatiably that we didn't emerge from her room for two days.

The following week I was sitting on her windowsill on a wet, humid Queensland day in New Farm being photographed wearing a crumpled black linen shirt and nothing on below. One of her photos from that session – from the waist up – was used as my SBS publicity shot for years afterwards. We were so smitten after a week together we even arranged a dinner to announce to her friends and family that she was moving in with me. I phoned back home to tell everyone what was happening and quickly flew back to Sydney to look for a bigger apartment. I started contacting real estate agents. I couldn't believe how blessed I'd been to land such a fantastic woman so soon after the end of my marriage – and nor could Giancarlo, who was unable to contain his jealousy when I took her for lunch at Piazzolla. She possessed everything he desired in a woman.

'What's the best way I can put this?' he said when she went to the bathroom. 'I want to kill you, Fink.'

My karma was good. I was striking a blow for jilted men everywhere. But then, without warning, Chloe called it off.

'I'm sorry, Jesse. I cannot physically and emotionally give the time that is needed to have a relationship,' she told me by email after I hadn't heard from her for a few days and had started to worry.

Thankfully Lara had steeled me for the caprice of women.

A year went past without so much as a word and I'd begun dating other women when Chloe decided to send me a text message. She said she was sorry and wanted to see me. She'd broken off an engagement with a Frenchman and was single. She'd be in Sydney for a weekend. Could she meet me?

I said yes. We again made athletic, sweaty love at her hotel, throwing each other across the suite with the abandon of Keith Moon smashing a drum kit. It was like we'd never broken up. She was now living in South Australia and asked me to come to Adelaide and stay with her for a weekend. Looking into her eyes and seeing that old fire inside, I thought we might have a second chance.

Chloe was a woman who took pride in the fact she took chances. As well as Tuva, she'd travelled to the Hindu Kush and the forgotten reaches of the bombed-out Pacific, where no tourists went, to document stories the world didn't want to know about. But although she could confidently walk past a cordon of Taliban soldiers she ran scared from long-term relationships. I was in the process of booking my flight when I tried to contact her over some minor travel detail and encountered the same inexplicable *volte-face*. She'd gone to ground again.

'I don't want you to come. There was a reason why it didn't work the first time,' she said coldly when I got through to her on the phone after several attempts.

I hung up on her, absolutely furious, and we didn't speak another word to each other. Once more, I got on with my life and saw other women.

But like clockwork, another 12 months later, she got in touch again. She was in a faltering relationship with a man she said she loved yet had no hesitation in sending me an Instagram photo of herself completely naked.

Chloe was in fine shape and looked amazing but it was beside the point. When I asked why she felt it necessary to send such a picture on her phone, after everything that had happened, after abandoning me twice, all she could say was: 'I had to get your attention somehow.'

It turned out her new lover had been distant with her and was avoiding commitment. He'd been canvassing the idea of group sex, which she was resisting. When she went through his phone and checked some of the dialled numbers, she discovered he was calling gay chat lines. She confronted him and he admitted he'd been leading a double life. He was having sex with transvestites.

Chloe had been contemplating breaking it off with him for months. Now, with these latest revelations, I suggested it was a *fait accompli*. The relationship wasn't likely to get better and his shift away from heterosexuality wasn't miraculously going to stop.

'Dump him, Chloe.'

'You *think*? I'm so torn.'

'What are you? Fucking mad? Do it.'

'Okay. I will. You've convinced me.'

I was going to Adelaide for a business trip. Chloe assured me she'd finally grown up. Could we try one last time? I warned her I'd cut her out of my life altogether if she ran off on me again. She agreed we had chemistry. That part was unavoidable.

'I want us to connect,' I said.

'As lovers?' she replied.

'We should be together.'

'We should, Fink.'

It was happening all over again. Chloe even sent me a text that knocked me off my feet but should have started ringing alarm bells: 'I know we have something special. I felt it after hearing your voice the other night. Impregnate me. I want to have your child, Jesse.'

TURBULENCE ADDICTION

But a few days before leaving for Adelaide, she went cold on me again, rolling out excuses for not meeting. She'd got back with her tranny-fucking boyfriend.

'But he *loves* me. I never said I wanted to have a relationship with you, Jesse. I just thought we could have some fun. But you want *more*.'

Three strikes.

* * *

With Marguerite I got lucky. I say lucky because she was tormented, volatile, impossible and incendiary, a veritable Lisbeth Salander: all the things that, coupled with her physical beauty and god-given figure, made this woman, in my eyes at the time, the most fuckable creature in the universe.

A striking black-maned novelist in her 40s with a penchant for bad 1980s hair metal and in possession of titanic breasts that would have roused Russ Meyer from his eternal rest, she'd recently returned to Sydney after a couple of years in Portugal, where her marriage to her first husband had started falling apart not long after they'd moved there.

A Portuguese speaker, he'd adapted to his new job as a TV director. A monolingual Australian girl from the suburbs, she hadn't. He eventually drifted off and had an affair. The relationship ended. She came home, grieving, like me flattened to the point of suicide, and fell into a short-lived relationship with a drug addict. She'd weaned him off ice and then promptly left him. Another rescuer. When we met online, her husband was marrying the mistress, which had sent her off the deep end.

As writers, we clicked. Marguerite was getting her third book published and nursing a fat advance from her publisher, which allowed her to live in an austere, whitewashed, minimalist cliffside apartment in Coogee, a beach suburb east of Darlinghurst. But better, we shared a rare appreciation for yacht rock, that much maligned genre of smooth music from the late 1970s/early '80s that had given rise to Michael McDonald, Hall & Oates, Christopher Cross and Pablo Cruise.

Almost every day I'd go to Marguerite's flat and we'd fuck every which way for hours, interpolating our sessions with discussions about the artistic merits of Def Leppard, the DeFranco Family and 'Stumblin' In', Chris Norman from Smokie's lamentable duet with Suzi Quatro. Marguerite was the only known woman in the history of rock who'd turned down Sebastian Bach. The towering Skid Row singer, one of the great ladies' men of the 1980s, had dropped his drawers in his hotel room on a visit to Sydney and dangled his cock in her face. Rather than take his member, she'd burst out laughing.

TURBULENCE ADDICTION

Our maladaptive personalities were sparking with our jealousies and insecurities, with our sadness at losing our marriages, with our desperate need to be touched. The problem was when the sex was over it was no different. We fought like cornered animals. When I craved intimacy, Marguerite wasn't prepared to give it. When she wanted nurturing, I wasn't able to provide it. She didn't want me to be her boyfriend but also couldn't handle it when I withdrew or backed off.

She accused me of being controlling yet determined when and where I saw her and under what conditions and gave me completely mixed signals the entire time I was with her. It was either a case of *You're amazing, I really want to fuck your brains out* or *I can't stand you, get the fuck out of my life.*

Her wish was that we would be allies, platonic life rafts to help each other get to a point of emotional safety, yet the sex complicated us getting anywhere near that destination because it was unaccountably more than either of us could have wished for. She wanted it in the arse. She'd suck and work on my cock like she was squeezing the last dregs of juice out of a Calippo. She could go for hours. She was beautiful. Marguerite was that rare female every man hopes to meet: one to happily fuck for the rest of your life.

But she wouldn't let me forget my past. Not so much the cataclysm with Lara. More the first dates and one-night stands that came after her, what she pejoratively called 'The Others'.

To her mind I was too uncommitted, too wayward, too chronically fucked up to consider for a serious relationship. She felt, rightly, that I was treating her like a whore, not a potential girlfriend. When I wasn't with her I was prowling bars, beaches and dating sites, 'reeling in all the gash'. And she wasn't far wrong. I was still using sex to outrun my demons.

'Throwing your fucking genitals into a collection to be hopefully extracted as the lucky door prize isn't all that appealing,' she rejoindered when I proposed commitment, cutting me down to size with a perfectly selected metaphor.

'But Margie, I think we've got a really good thing going on.'

'I love what we have. But I'm not ready for more than this. You're not either. I need more time and it's not fair of me to expect you to wait around while I figure out what I want and whether you're the man I want to be with.'

Waiting was not a word I wanted to hear. But she was right. I wasn't ready. She wasn't ready. I was in love with another woman. She was in love with another man. What we felt we had wasn't love. It was *need*. And we would have most certainly killed each other had we moved in together.

We agreed to end it.

There are some love affairs that appear unstoppable but burn out quickly like a rocket re-entering the atmosphere and this was one of them. Marguerite and I had met in the wrong place at the wrong time. Or perhaps we hadn't. Maybe it just was what it was. Maybe we'd got more out of it than we should have and were fortunate to have had this small window of time together.

I saw very little of her after that. I hit her up from time to time for casual sex but she didn't want to go down that path and we naturally drifted apart.

We saw each other one last time, by accident, when I walked past the window of a crowded pub in Darlinghurst and she was inside drinking with some friends. I tapped on the glass. She came out and gave me a hug and then went back inside. I stood for a moment watching her talk. After having shared so much together – screaming matches, fits of laughter, tears, some of the best sex of our lives – it felt like I was looking at a stranger.

But that's what love – or a feeling we mistake for love – can be like. Two people come into each other's lives by chance, they change each other, and then just as quickly they recede before going off to do the same thing with someone else.

We disappear. We are not important. We are inconsequential. We leave very little behind. We are, as we have always been and will always be, just random atoms bumping into each other in the vast timelessness of space.

* * *

Frankie, the last of the trio, was the biggest mindfuck of all. Stunningly beautiful, chronically shy, socially awkward, jealous, indulged and afflicted with Asperger's syndrome, she would end up hurting me even more than Lara had. Would drive me more insane than Chloe and Marguerite. Our relationship would push me to the edge of my sanity and shine a light on dark corners of my mind that truly terrified me.

As crazy as she was, Frankie would change my life and make me understand what I saw as the true nature of romantic love or 'limerence' or whatever the term *du jour* is for that feeling we all know and search our whole lives for but find hard to adequately describe. Something far different from the love I'd been told about at my wedding.

Due to my dating failures and inability to have, let alone hold down, a relationship post Lara, I had started to suspect love was just a rush some of us experience in our youth when we haven't yet been hurt. In our 20s we're inexperienced in relationships, we haven't seen a lot of the world, we don't know much real disappointment and pain, we're carried away on this zephyr of lust and adrenalin from meeting someone we want to fuck badly and who wants to fuck us badly, feelings get jumbled up amid the fucking, we marry too soon when we're not anywhere near ready for that kind of commitment and ultimately we pay for it like the suckers we are.

TURBULENCE ADDICTION

Frankie blew that theory to bits. Though she was maddening, sometimes cruel, habitually unwell and totally impossible to live with, I was head over. Completely addicted to the danger I was in just being around her, never knowing when she was going to lash out wildly, call the cops or grab me by the neck and kiss me.

I thought I was the luckiest man in the world.

At various times in her adult life she'd been a surfer chick, a goth and a raver, flitting between California and Australia with her two passports. Now she was a painter, a recluse with gallery representation, living rent-free in her parents' investment apartment down by the harbour in Elizabeth Bay.

She hoarded toothbrushes and white T-shirts. She slept on the living-room floor because she felt safer there than in bed. She could hide in her apartment for days, surviving on bunker rations of tea and dry biscuits and listening to shitty music like Mika on repeat.

She threw out expensive thick towels and replaced them with cheap thin ones. She had a single dark hair growing out of one of her cheeks, which she refused to pluck.

She had tiny ears, like a child's, and long fingers, like a golem's, with full-sized legs and a shortened middle. (She should have been 5'11" but was 5'6", anorexia during puberty having stunted her growth.)

She had a rare ability to paint anything and make it beautiful: hills, clouds, highways. She could turn out whole series of oil paintings of mundane, everyday objects like slabs of supermarket meat, screwed-up dollar notes, boxes of matches. She had the willowy looks of a Ralph Lauren catalogue model but the aesthetics of someone who dressed in the dark.

Yet it all worked. When she walked up the main street of Potts Point each morning on her way to the art stores and galleries of Paddington, Frankie couldn't be mistaken for anyone else. She wore scarves even on the hottest days. She cut off striped socks at the ankles and wore them on her arms. She bought Italian leather boots and painted the buckles purple and orange. She made her own style. She was her own creation. She imitated nobody. One look at her was enough to lift my heart and forget all my pain. She'd given me what one of my favourite writers, Stephen Vizinczey, had described in his 1965 novel *In Praise of Older Women: The Amorous Recollections of András Vajda* as 'an emotional glimpse of eternity'.

It wasn't supposed to happen. Not to me. Not now. But the feeling was unmistakable. I was in love.

CHAPTER 7

BAD FATHER

TRACK 7 'Amoreena', Elton John,
Tumbleweed Connection (1970)

The vexing issue of my love affair with Frankie was that I still yearned for my ex-wife. Whenever I looked at the face of my daughter, with her little ski-jump nose, high cheekbones, big eyes and wide smile, I saw Lara. Seeing Evie almost always involved some discomfort in that way. It was a bittersweet, anguished, guilty feeling and familiar to other divorced men I'd spoken to. You try to block out any picture of your ex in your mind but you are constantly reminded of her when you're with your child.

When I saw Evie it just brought home how much I missed Lara and the short time the three of us had had together. How I'd lost the chance to bring to life the Norman Rockwell vision I'd had of our future: Lara, growing more beautiful as she got older, helping a teenage Evie do her homework at the kitchen table; me, a bit of grey in my beard, glasses on the end of my nose, cooking dinner for all of us; Bosco lying at the foot of our bed when we turned in for the night. Standing side by side at our daughter's wedding, giving her away. Toasting our first grandchild. Celebrating our 50th anniversary. Perhaps even making a pact in our old age to die together because we couldn't ever bear to be apart. All pretty basic wishes.

I didn't have that. I had the single father's consolation prize: awkward phone calls after dinner.

'How was your day, Evie?'

'Good.'

'Anything happen?'

'Nup.'

'How's Mum?'

'Good.'

'Well, I just rang to say I love you.'

'I love you, too, Dad.'

Click. This wasn't what I'd signed up for.

But together Frankie and Evie also looked like mother and daughter. People commented how alike they were and how lucky I was to have such a beautiful family. Evie, now six, adored Frankie. She began dressing like her. She started using her make-up. We'd go out together to wine bars, all dressed up, Evie drinking pink lemonade while we drank Klur from Alsace. She even reported to Lara how happy Daddy was and how pretty his new girlfriend was.

I secretly took great pleasure in this. If Lara had one weakness it was her vanity; like many beautiful women she was insecure. She was used to being the most attractive girl in the room, the one everyone looked at and desired. Suddenly she had competition and her ex-husband didn't seem to be so cut up anymore. The texts and emails had stopped. The conversations at handovers had got shorter. Not coincidentally, I felt, she began taking an interest in what I was doing with my life, acting for the first time in years like I actually existed.

It made me angry. We were divorced by then. Though reconciliation had never been mentioned I got the feeling all wasn't well in her relationship with David and she was having misgivings. But if she were to offer a way back (something she had always been adamant would never happen) I wasn't going to give up what I had now, even when Lara was the only way I would ever recover the whole. My new girlfriend made me let go of that. We had something romantic and special of our own, even if, unflatteringly, she insisted on clipping my ear hair or forced me into a chair to scrape tartar from my teeth. As a dentist's daughter she'd learned a few things.

Yet Frankie wasn't comfortable being cast in the role of stepmother. When she asked to see photos of Lara I could read her face. She didn't trust me. She didn't believe that I wouldn't go back to my ex-wife if the opportunity arose, even though we had papers that said we were no longer recognised in law as a couple. That created the conditions for anger, paranoia, jealousy, anxiety, insecurity and flammability to enter our relationship – the very toxins any relationship is lucky to survive, let alone one with a diagnosed 'Aspy' who stubbornly refused to see herself as such and who didn't want to take medication.

Frankie fitted the criteria perfectly. She didn't understand emotions or facial expressions. She didn't have a normal capacity for empathy. She couldn't look me in the eye because she wasn't able to deal with intimacy. She didn't like to be touched without warning. She had regular turns in which she retreated into her shell and shunned all social activity. She felt more affinity with insects and other small creatures than she did people.

Her life was her painting, her routine.

'I do similar things every day if I can,' she once told me. 'If I could do them without ever having to see another human again I would.'

* * *

BAD FATHER

I first saw just how volatile my new girlfriend could be when one night Evie and I stayed over at her flat, a small space with little natural light filled floor to ceiling with her father's grim collection of Indonesian and Melanesian tribal masks.

When Evie accidentally knocked over a cup of tea that had been left on the carpeted floor, spilling on to a cow-skin rug, Frankie screamed at me from the kitchen.

'Put *WATER* on it!'

I did as I was told, picking it up and scampering to the bathroom where I stood it under a running shower. When Frankie followed me in and saw what I was doing, something misfired in her head.

'I said put it under a *tap*, not the shower! You've ruined it!'

'Calm down, Frankie. You said put water on it.'

'Are you fucking stupid? Give it to me. Get out. Leave!'

'Calm *down*!'

Evie was now in the bathroom. She looked distressed. Frankie was panicking.

'Get out! If you don't fucking go I'm going to call the police.'

'What the fuck? Frankie, calm the fuck down!'

Evie had started crying. The word 'police' had revived a long-buried trauma. She'd been there when David had choked me. She was frightened.

'Dad, *Dad*! Are the police coming?'

'Evie, everything's alright. Frankie, stop it. You're scaring Evie.'

'You're scaring both of us. Get out! That's *it*!'

Frankie ran into the living room, picked up the cordless phone from its charger stand and began dialling the police. I went after her and grabbed it. By now Evie was sobbing – my little girl had clearly seen too much when David and I had come to blows – and her reaction was the only thing that defused what could have been a nasty situation. It stopped Frankie in her tracks.

An hour later, everything was normal. Evie and I were sitting on the couch eating our dinner, Frankie was in the middle of the floor, where she liked to be, curled up in a blanket, watching TV, and the cow-skin rug was drying on the shower rod. Undamaged. Good as new. But I'd been given a taste of how hard it can be to love someone with a disorder.

With Frankie I was always walking on eggshells, constantly worrying about whether a simple look might make her walk away from me on the street or if something I said would see her hide from me for days, not returning my phone calls. Once, when I was admonishing her over something insignificant, she sprayed insecticide in my face. Didn't think twice about it.

'What the fuck did you do that for?' I stammered, my eyes bloodshot and stinging.

'You deserved it.'

But I was punch drunk on her talent and beauty. I couldn't get enough of her. If her space was so important, then why not give her one that we could both share happily? That was ours. Not her dad's. A space she could fill with all the paintings, chewed-up old kilims and stacks of neatly folded white laundry she liked. A place where she could paint and I could write and we could live together happily forever and never have to be away from each other, like Paul and Linda McCartney.

So I asked Frankie to move in with me. She agreed. It was just about the single dumbest thing I could have done.

* * *

It started out alright. We got a new apartment at the bottom of a terrace right around the corner from Piazzolla. We were right in the thick of things. We went shopping together and bought new stuff for the flat, as all couples do. Frankie set up a part of the living room as her painting area and put up a partition, behind which she could retreat and lie down with a blanket and some pillows when she was sick of looking at me. She even painted a magnificent oil portrait of Evie, the height of a wall, my daughter's hair ablaze with thick brushstrokes of red, pink, orange, white and violet like the lick of a bushfire. It took pride of place in our home. At night we cooked together, watched movies together, slept together. All normal. But then my OCD struck again with a vengeance.

The act of nesting with Frankie and coming closer with her emotionally and physically gave my OCD new purpose. It was determined to destroy me. The feeling of being in love and being drawn to her made it worse.

So when one evening while Frankie was chopping carrots in the kitchen I had an image flash through my mind of stabbing her in the neck, OCD had made its intentions clear. We'd make love tenderly and disturbing thoughts would come into my head at the point of orgasm. It was debilitating, endless. And the most tormenting part was that I couldn't keep it to myself.

A big part of my OCD is a need to confess, to get reassurance. So, just as with Lara, I told Frankie everything. It was a mark of her compassion and goodness that she listened and didn't judge me, even when what I was saying was deeply confronting. She came with me to see my therapist so we could learn how to deal with it as a united front. Eventually we agreed I didn't have to tell her the content of my obsessions – the psych recommended it – and things did get better with everything out in the open, but it was a constant struggle.

When I went on a work trip to Malaysia my mind caved in on itself. I became deeply worried over having let Evie sit on my knee before I'd left and began thinking this normal, fatherly action had somehow been inappropriate. (There's a reason OCD is called the 'doubting disease'. You doubt *everything*.) The whole notion was ridiculous – rationally I understood that – but such irrational thoughts escalate in the grip of OCD until they become full-blown obsessions and push you to the brink of losing your grip on reality.

Alone, confused and utterly anguished in an air-conditioned shopping mall at the Petronas Towers in Kuala Lumpur, surrounded by faceless women in their *tudungs* and faceless men in their *taqiyahs*, I stood by a ledge contemplating throwing myself off the top level and onto the marble six floors below. But instead of jumping I turned away, found a leather sofa, sat down and burst into tears.

A security guard asked me to get up and leave.

That same night, I appeared as a guest on a TV chat show live across South-East Asia, garrulous, effusive, making jokes, and nobody in the world knew what I was going through.

But, as with all private torments, whoever does?

* * *

Back in Australia, Frankie, Evie and I went on a planned summer holiday with Alby, his wife, Penny, and the rest of my family to Hawks Nest, a popular resort town on the New South Wales mid-north coast. There were kids everywhere and I was still in the grip of the most terrible OCD episode of my life, a simple glance at any of the people I loved triggering disturbing thoughts. The more I tried to ignore them the more malignant and persistent they became.

So I did what the therapist told me to do and exposed myself to the worst of the thoughts, even deliberately conjured them, the idea being greater frequency of the thoughts would habituate me to them and reduce the anxiety. This was exposure and response prevention in action. But it wasn't helping. I was in a place of unrelenting torment, taking long walks on the beach just to get away from everybody and not wanting to bother Frankie with my problems.

At breakfast one morning all the kids were seated at the dining table. I walked in to face my fears.

'Evie, would you like a glass of water?'

'Thanks, Dad,' she said, and I went off to the kitchen, filled her a glass of water and brought it back to the table. So far, so good.

My sister, Tammy, piped up. She was sitting on a nearby sofa. 'Why didn't you ask the others if they wanted water?'

'Sorry, honestly, I didn't think to ask,' I replied.

BAD FATHER

'Well, that's typical. Because you're a bad father.'

The words cut me deeper than anything Lara had said when she walked out on me. Tammy had said them in front of my daughter, the person I loved more than anything in the world and would do anything for. I lived for her. I *struggled to live* for her. She'd said them in front of my girlfriend, the woman I hoped would be my next wife and give me a new family. She'd said them in front of my father, my stepmother, my brother-in-law, my niece and my nephew. She'd also said them when I was trying to fight off the OCD and do for Evie what I hadn't been able to do so many times for Lara and Frankie: be there in the moment. Tammy wasn't to know what I was going through and perhaps rightly felt aggrieved because earlier that day I'd taken to walking off at a moment's notice with Frankie, leaving her to take care of Evie, but I didn't have the presence of mind at the time to see the situation from her side.

My mind was a jumble of scenes. I was back at Balmoral, trying to stop my parents fighting. I was back at Lara's flat, screaming into the door. I was back at the mall in KL, looking over the ledge. I wasn't in the moment, I was downloading all the bad static of my past and it was coursing through me, a lifetime of traumas unspooling in my head.

When it came, the anger that erupted from me felt like it was three decades in the making. All the resentments I had for the women in my life – Sal, Tammy, Penny, Lara – came spewing out of my mouth. I chased my sister around the house, my thoughts scrambled, my voice faltering, my body shaking, my fists pounding on the walls. Pure, unhinged fury. Terrifying everyone, but especially myself. There was so much hurt inside me. I was out of control.

When it was over, I just slumped, my head in my hands, and disintegrated. I had nothing left inside me.

Alby came up to me and said it plainly: 'You've just ended your relationship. Well done, son.'

* * *

I knew Alby was right, even though Frankie assured me everything was going to be okay and she knew just how loaded and fractured my family history was; hers was just as bad. Her father and brother had what she suspected was borderline personality disorder and she'd had a strained relationship with her father all her life. We drove back to Sydney, me swearing never to see my family again, Frankie preparing her exit strategy.

It didn't take long for it to be executed. I'd organised a job for her through a French friend, Arnon. She'd be working a couple of nights a week at his wine bar, not far from where we lived, making cocktails, cleaning glasses. The first night went well. I turned up at 1am when she was finishing up her shift and we shared a bottle of wine. The second night she didn't come home.

Frankie was back at her parents' apartment, hiding something from me. I kept pushing and eventually she told me the truth. She'd left with a waiter, Emile, who'd been working at the bar and stayed out drinking with him till 6am. Another Frenchman. They'd kissed but she maintained they hadn't slept together. (I'd heard that before.) When I later ran into Arnon on the street, he was apologetic and seemed genuinely shocked.

'She wasn't even attracted to him,' he said.

Frankie confirmed she'd done it just to get away from me and didn't know the best way how. Emile had suited her purposes.

I didn't feel like a person anymore. I was broken. The fight with Tammy at Hawks Nest, the recrudescing OCD and now Frankie's infidelity had rubbed me out. I needed to *feel* something. That old urge to fuck returned. But I didn't want to go on a date. I didn't have the patience. All my former booty calls had retired into relationships.

So I went to a massage parlour.

* * *

I'd never been to a 'rub 'n' tug' joint, as Australians call them. The idea had previously repelled me. Now, short of enlisting the services of a hooker, it seemed like the only choice I had. I walked into an unassuming terrace in East Sydney, put some money down and, with a strange mix of self-loathing and anticipation, chose a woman to pleasure me.

Xanthe was a goddess: blonde, tanned, fit, with incredible pornstar breasts and an authentic, smoky sexuality I'd only ever come across before in Lara and Marguerite. In the candlelight of the small room, looking down the topography of my naked body to where her kohl-smudged eyes and my cock met, I felt like I'd been transported to a mughal's bed chamber. All for $180. That hour made me forget about all my tumult. Far from being awful and sad, it was the most erotic experience I could have hoped for.

What was awful and sad was my timing. The next day Frankie wanted to get back together. She was remorseful about what had happened with Emile, but in those 24 hours I'd gone out and deposited my semen between a sex worker's tits. I'd learned nothing from my past. I should have resisted the idea to confess, like I had to Lara over Brooke – this was my chance to take the moral high ground, get some leverage – but I had OCD. I couldn't live with the idea of harbouring a secret, even though technically I'd been a single man when it happened.

BAD FATHER

So I told her the full story.

It couldn't have gone any worse. Frankie's palpable horror was mitigated by her own indiscretion, but she left on the next train for her parents' country property and told me not to even try contacting her.

'You're disgusting,' she said, as if I were a smear of shit on the sole of her Birkenstocks.

I was heartbroken.

Two weeks later she returned to Darlinghurst in a more conciliatory mood – her mother, the only 'normal' member of her family, had told her she was overreacting – and we tried to make things work again but we'd both created too many breaches in our relationship. It was too late.

When she was invited to a boozy painting weekend in the Southern Highlands with a painter ex-boyfriend and a clutch of his single painter mates, she thought nothing of the danger it presented to our relationship. I didn't want her to go. I was insecure and jealous. But Frankie didn't give a damn. She'd already mentally checked out. She gathered up the few things that remained in the flat, took what she could carry, told me to go to hell and slammed the door on the way out.

* * *

I went back to licking my wounds in the best way I knew how – sex – and tried to convince myself I'd dodged a bullet even though I felt that I'd lost the true love of my life. Frankie blocked me on Facebook, changed her number and went and found another man, Jacob, a nature photographer and trust-fund baby who lived in an enormous mansion in Vaucluse with his elderly widowed mother.

Occasionally we'd run into each other on the street and when I tried to talk to her she'd walk straight past me like I was a hawker handing out flyers. Another time I reached out to her on the main street of Potts Point with my hand and she let out a horrible shriek like I'd tried to sexually assault her. Within earshot of hundreds of people. Mostly she'd acknowledge me with a glance and just keep walking. But I had a part of her: the painting of Evie. It was the centrepiece of my apartment, the one possession I had of any real value, financially and emotionally; Frankie's bigger paintings sold for near $10,000. It was a picture of my daughter based on one of my photographs and from a time that was special to me in so many ways. A time when I genuinely felt there was life after Lara.

But after months of rejecting my letters beseeching her to come back and several more disastrous approaches on the street, Frankie emailed me and said she wanted the painting back for a group show of large works. She needed to have it photographed to enter some art prizes she'd missed out on the previous year.

I couldn't believe it. I regarded it as mine. I didn't want it going anywhere, whether it was her intention to photograph it, hang it, enter it, sell it, take it back or return it to me. I most certainly didn't want to run the risk of seeing it hanging in someone else's house, like another one of her paintings of my nephew, Isaac.

She didn't see it that way.

'I want to show it. I'll get someone to pick it up. I can do a smaller one to suit your taste,' she said.

The issue elicited two wildly diverging opinions from my friends and family. One, that morally I was the owner of the painting and I'd never see it returned. Two, that the painting, morally or otherwise, would always be Frankie's. That it had never been sold to me and as its creator she was entitled to take it back. Alby, who was a painter himself, implored me to hand it over, saying I had the opportunity to do the right thing and show I was bigger than her; it was just a painting. I argued and prevaricated, but he was right. It was an object. Just another thing. Not a memory or a feeling. And so I gave it back. I let it go.

Something I had to learn to do when it came to love.

* * *

Romantic love is, as Stephen Vizinczey says, an emotional glimpse of eternity. A moment of beauty and fulfilment when time doesn't seem to exist. An overwhelming feeling that can't be measured like a standard drink. When a simple look at a person can engorge you with a thousand emotions, dislodging you from the temporal world and its mundanities. It's when you know you're 'in love'. Frankie gave me a constellation of these glimpses.

The way her mouth opened slightly when she came. The way she looked wearing nothing but a cheap white T-shirt. The way she tied her hair up at the back when she painted. The way she called cheap grog 'goon'. The way she cried when she told me about growing up at boarding schools, being bullied by other girls for being different and not getting the sort of love she, and all children, deserve.

Relationships can be confused with love. They can be stalks of companionship with tendrils connecting us to glimpses. If we don't get enough of these glimpses, we leave relationships or we stay in loveless ones, hoping they will come.

But we all live for just a few moments of love. And we should be happy for any of these glimpses of eternity, even if they are fleeting. It's why, after loving and losing Frankie, I came to forgive her. I also came to forgive Lara. I learned to be grateful for the special moments I had with both of them and getting to experience what I felt was real love. And the miracle: I'd found it through a dating site the second time around with Frankie.

It takes true courage to accept and let go of a relationship when those moments don't happen anymore and knowing the difference between showing loyalty and being in love. The two women I loved made that decision for me both times but they were right to do so. You must always take the risk of moving on. There is nobility in learning to be with yourself and opening up to the possibility of more glimpses, whether that solitude comes through your own design or by being forced upon you.

Love is the secret of being alive. It is life.

* * *

Two years after breaking up with this turbulent but unforgettable woman, Evie and I went to the Wayside Chapel op-shop in Kings Cross where Frankie and I had spent so much of our time together, sorting cotton grades of white T-shirts, collecting scarves. It was late in the afternoon. I went to one corner of the room and began filing through the jeans rack. Evie went to the other to have a look around. A few moments later, I felt a tug on my arm. It was a small hand.

'Dad, these are Frankie's,' Evie said, looking up and showing me two little unsigned oil studies of purple flowers painted on scraps of tin. She was so happy and pleased with herself for spotting their quality. The shop assistants hadn't. My daughter wanted a little memento of Frankie too.

We paid for them – $2 a pop – walked out and, like we had so many times before, started talking about what we were going to have for dinner.

CHAPTER 8

SMALL WORLD

TRACK 8 'Rock 'n' Roll Damnation', AC/DC, *Powerage* (1978)

In an age when we've never had so much choice about where we can go, with faster planes flying to every point of the globe, increasingly we're spending our lives ungrounded and in transit. Just as we are in relationships. Frequently the love we encounter is as modified for modern life as the movies we watch at 35,000 feet.

As the seats on planes get more gizmos stuffed into them to distract us from contemplating the yawning blue terror outside, the implicit promise of technology is to spare us from the terror of solitude. But shit food will still get served up on planes as shit relationships will still get served up online. You can spend money to 'get away' but it's just an expensive way of taking your problems with you. A good profile photo on Facebook or a dating site might attract a lot of admirers or elicit endless friend requests from complete strangers but isn't going to change the fact that you still have to learn to live with yourself.

I say this with conviction now, but after the breakdown of my relationship with Frankie I had yet to accept these truths. I had lost the only woman who had ever really meant anything to me other than my ex-wife and my attempts to find a replacement for her seemed futile. The problem was that the bar had been set higher. Nearly three years after our break-up, Lara was now no longer so much of an issue. Rather the girls I was meeting in Sydney didn't come anywhere near to approximating what I would need to get over Frankie.

I was cursed, as a lot of men are, by having met a woman who was so unique and lovely that all who came after her seemed inadequate. I couldn't help judging them against Frankie and they always came up short. Not interesting enough. Not intelligent enough. Not sexy enough. Arse too big. Arms too fat. Men the world over are afflicted with this blight on their reason. We might marry plainer women, have kids with them, but we are corrupted forever if a beautiful woman chooses us. It's like a blue ribbon for our ego. We are good enough for her. Thereafter what's good enough for us can never be the same. And if that beautiful woman leaves, we labour under the mistaken belief that every other beautiful woman will find us just as appealing. Frequently, the very opposite applies. It's a humiliating wake-up call. The truth is we just got lucky. Physical beauty isn't forever. We need to revise our expectations, get real, be less superficial and prepare to be surprised by beauty that comes from the inside. But so many men don't. So they stay single, hoping to meet the girl with the megawatt smile and pornstar rack who's going to put everything right and clinically discard those who don't meet their personal benchmark. Or they accept someone less desirable and will tell their friends they're content when the reality is they're not. They think about other women when they're fucking. They masturbate to porn. They'll ask for the blindfold in bed because they're sick to death of looking at the woman they settled on and need that fantasy woman in their heads to be able to come. We men really can be the most pathetic creatures.

As for me, the inveterate fool, I had chosen to be single and not settle. I accepted the corollary of more loneliness. I didn't want to date for the sake of just getting laid. I had done enough of that and it didn't bring me any pleasure entering situations with women knowing that my heart wasn't in it and I was just going through the motions for the sake of human contact. I'd dated half the female population of Sydney anyway before I'd started going out with Frankie and many of those women were right in thinking I'd been a shallow, selfish prick. They hadn't seen me at my best.

I'd had a few interstate affairs but it wasn't until after Frankie had walked out on me and I was having trouble dealing with not having her in my life that I suddenly twigged I hadn't tried looking for The One overseas. I'd fielded a couple of emails from abroad when my profile was up on local dating sites, including one from Taylor, a big-lipped Angeleño who'd broken up with a Hollywood-based Australian daytime soapie star, but had never sent furtive solicitations the other way.

It made perfect sense. We live in a world more connected than ever before. Airline travel has never been cheaper. If you're not a bearded cleric from Waziristan or Java, visas are easier to get than at any other time, if not waived altogether. People fall in love on Facebook. Circumstances change. Lives can start over somewhere else. The only hitch to meeting, mating and keeping a woman was my parental status. I'd have to find a girl who'd be happy to move to Australia and put up with Evie crawling into our bed in the middle of the night.

* * *

SMALL WORLD

When I saw Olivia's profile, 'Cambridge Pairs', on the *Guardian*'s personals site, I knew we already had a connection – we just hadn't met. I think that's how it is sometimes when you see the face of a stranger in a photo. There's already a kind of shared history between you. The depth in someone's eyes. The laugh lines on their face. The way they dress. I knew instinctively the first time I saw Olivia that we had to meet, even though she lived in Cambridge, Massachusetts, the university town just across the river from Boston.

She was English, had blonde straight hair that was cut short, soft full lips, a slender body, thick eyebrows that uncannily presaged the thick eyebrow craze of 2011, and beautiful clavicles. Physically she was not unlike Scarlett Johansson. If I could get a reply from her, I'd be doing very well for myself. But what really excited me about Olivia was her work: she was a psychiatrist *and* a burlesque dancer. (Cambridge Pairs, I was later to discover, was a stage name that referred to her ample breasts.) She was the composite of everything I desired: a sex bomb who could write a prescription.

I wrote to her and almost instantly received a reply. Within an hour, we were Skyping – me lying back on my bed in Sydney, Olivia on her living-room floor in Cambridge. Apart from 16,000 kilometres, nothing separated us. The ease of the conversation, our shared grievances (she, too, was recovering from a bad divorce) and the excruciating attraction we were both feeling (wanting to reach out and touch one another but finding only an LED-backlit display) made it very hard to press the little red hang-up button. Even after six hours. We talked so much that when we ran out of things to say we just looked at each other for long stretches and sighed. It was like being 15 again.

The next day she emailed me from her university department.

'I can't stop thinking about you. I'm sitting at my desk, having arrived an hour and a half late, unable to focus on anything, soaking wet because it's pouring with rain and I ran outside without an umbrella or hat, and my heart is doing flips. Are we crazy? Did that all really happen? I had a reasonably normal life just 24 hours ago. You came along and flipped it on its head.

'It feels like I was drunk and probably not myself last night, except I wasn't drunk, and I can't recall if at some point I've crossed the line from being normal and went straight to insane. Or if it's at all possible to fall in love with a stranger via the internet via Skype.'

In my experience, it's not. But it sure can feel that way.

* * *

SMALL WORLD

It was April 2010. Olivia had agreed to meet me in New York City, a place I'd fantasised about ever since I'd seen *Manhattan* as a teenager. That movie forever changed my life, my outlook, my ideas about love. More than anything else, it made me want to be a writer. There has never been a better ending to a film than when a teenage Mariel Hemingway faces off with a panting, middle-aged Woody Allen, who has just run across town to stop her from leaving to go to acting school in London, thinking he'll lose her for good, and she tells him before stepping into a car to catch her plane, 'Not everybody gets corrupted. You have to have a little faith in people.' Allen shoots her a look of wistful disappointment yet quiet acceptance, and smiles. The strings and horns of George Gershwin's 'Rhapsody in Blue' gather in the background, the action cuts away to three moody shots of the Manhattan skyline and the credits roll. I wanted my arrival at John F. Kennedy International Airport after the 20-hour trip from Sydney to be just as romantic and cinematic.

Instead of a Woody Allen movie I got the *Bang Bus*. Olivia unbuckled my jeans and pulled out my cock while we were driving on the Van Wyck Expressway into the city and didn't let go of it even when changing lanes. I put my hand inside her bra, then her vagina, which was hot and wet. The crotch of her black leggings was soaked. We couldn't keep our hands off each other. When we arrived in Manhattan and drove past the *New York Times* building on Eighth Avenue, she was holding on to me, stroking away. I was in some sort of incredible dream. I was in a lit-up New York, the adult Disneyland, with a girl who looked like one of the hottest actresses in Hollywood driving with one hand and getting me ready to come all over the dash with the other.

When we arrived in Hells Kitchen and checked into our hotel, we threw our bags down, tore at each other's clothes and fucked. But there was something missing. I couldn't quite place what it was about Olivia that wasn't right in my eyes but, while she was riding me, I didn't feel the all-consuming lust that should have been there. For about the first time in my life, I couldn't ejaculate. I made up some bullshit about being tired and not with it and suggested we go eat. This was not the way either of us had imagined it. And I was booked to stay in the States, specifically at Olivia's apartment, for a month.

After three days of avoiding sightseeing and trying to work things out in bed, we made the 300-kilometre drive to Cambridge. Olivia went back to her work. I explored Boston, Cambridge and the grounds of Harvard. At night we drank together in dive bars and fucked in her bedroom when we got home. But it wasn't happening, even though my feelings for her in real life were belatedly starting to catch up with how I'd felt about her online before I'd left Australia.

SMALL WORLD

She was, in every way, a great girl. I should have been happy. Unlike Frankie, she was empathetic. I told her all about my OCD and the turbulent relationship I'd just come out of. She'd been in one of her own, with an aggressive jock husband whose idea of lovemaking was to leave her feeling like she'd been raped. She was caring and considerate. She drove me around to Savers outlets so I could buy vintage T-shirts and took me to a Major League Soccer game at Gillette Stadium in Foxboro. We went back to New York for a weekend to see the 1970s prog-rock group Ambrosia in a bar in Brooklyn. She took me up to Rhode Island and the beautiful coast around Newport to scoff clams and drink beer. I was mistaken again for Robert Downey Jr when we stopped for lunch at a roadside café. Perhaps sensing our situation called for desperate measures, she even took me to the famous strip clubs of Providence and introduced me to the Foxy Lady, a hangout for the Rhode Island mafia with an interior and clientele straight out of a Martin Scorsese movie.

Sitting at the bar, peeling labels off the $3 beers, swatting away the covetous glances of the strippers, we got into an argument about burlesque versus stripping. Even though we'd come to the Foxy at Olivia's suggestion, and she assured me she'd frequented it several times with friends and loved the place, I sensed she was uncomfortable being there with me among the drunk servicemen and small-time gangsters.

Her hostility to the women working the room (or perhaps it was just me enjoying them that ticked her off) was palpable.

'If you didn't want to come why are we here?' I said.

'I thought you'd like it.'

'I *do* like it. So enjoy it with me, for Christ's sake. What they're doing and what you do are essentially no different, Olivia.'

'What are you talking about?'

'Sexual titillation.'

She looked at me like I'd hawked a gob of spit in her beer.

'I wish you could be here to see one of my shows. It's not about sexual titillation at all. It's about empowerment. About expression. Giving women back their bodies.'

'Horseshit,' I snapped, like the cocky arsehole I'd become. 'The only difference is you get lesbians and art students at your shows and that makes it somehow nobler.'

* * *

We returned to Cambridge in silence, but when we got back to her apartment I told her what I should have known all along: I was still in love with Frankie; the trip had been a mistake; if we had met in Australia things might have been different if we'd taken it slowly but we'd jumped in headfirst, way too fast. I hadn't meant to mislead her. I had genuinely wanted it to work and had come to America with every intention of taking her home with me.

Olivia took it well and said she'd known that we weren't right for each other but had tried to make it work, too. There were no hard feelings. She suggested we make the most of the time we had left. We made love and, mutually freed from pressure, it was the best sex we'd had together. But the rest of the week was tense – not helped by the fact one of her friends, Stella, an academic at Harvard, came on to me in a karaoke bar and, thinking all was okay between us and we were free to do as we pleased, I suggested a threesome. Olivia was appalled and hurt, even though Stella had kissed me. Bizarrely, they comforted each other while shooting death stares at me.

We stopped fucking.

So I used my free time to write an email to Frankie listing 100 things I missed about her. It took me hours and was one of the most heartfelt things I'd ever written to anybody.

1. Your need to have a pillow to hug in bed
26. The way your hair falls over your face
46. Your shameless torturing of older men who will never bed you
70. The way we held hands when I drove
77. Your fear of cold water
99. Just holding your waist

And so on.

But she responded without compassion: 'I know it's been hard but I'm not here to make life harder for you. Please, don't make me sad. You need someone to show you who's boss. And I'm not strong enough for you. I did love you for a while. I can't let you ruin my life. I can ruin it on my own.'

I was lost. Stuck in a university town outside Boston with a woman I didn't love who wanted me to leave, while at home the two women I loved didn't want a bar of me either. I had no one else but myself to blame. I'd been sucked into the vortex of disconnected love. The no-man's-land between real life and online fantasy, where distance doesn't matter but hopes and expectations of romance collide with the cold hard truth that very often life isn't very romantic at all. Effort and imagination have been replaced by laziness and automation. We don't need to fuck in real life anymore. We can do it on Skype.

Olivia drove me to Logan International Airport for the flight home. We kissed at the terminal and hugged. By the time I arrived home in Sydney she'd blocked me.

*　*　*

I hadn't regretted a moment of it. In a strange way the disaster with Olivia set my life on a totally different course that wouldn't have happened if I'd stayed trying to find love in Sydney. She opened up my eyes to the adventure life holds for all of us if we choose to take a chance and step away from what we know.

My mother had long intoned the mantra 'life begins after your first divorce' and previously it had aggravated the hell out of me. But Sal was right. I'd been re-energised sexually. I'd got back my physical health and returned to being the man I was before I'd transformed into the bearded cookie monster Lara had abandoned. I had fallen in love with another woman despite still loving my ex-wife. I'd been to places I never thought I'd see and met people – not least Giancarlo, Enrico, Kristin and Ron – who'd changed me for the better and given me a whole new appreciation of what was really important. And I'd only just begun.

There is something to be said for being dumped. It should happen to everyone at one point or another. So many of us try to save relationships that aren't working out of some misguided notion that trial and perseverance and not passion and ongoing compatibility are what really matters – what Dr Millikan said at my wedding to Lara. But trial and perseverance are good for durability, not necessarily for love. I would come to realise I had nothing to prove to my parents or anyone by being married to the one woman for perpetuity. Care, admiration and fidelity are good things and crucial to any relationship, but they shouldn't override elation and hunger. Lara had stopped having her glimpses of eternity with me. She was as entitled to make something of her life as I was mine. She hadn't signed up for my depression and OCD. Our marriage certificate wasn't a prison sentence. Evie had managed to overcome all that we had thrown at her and emerged a more rounded, switched-on child. She was happy. That was all that mattered. (Had we persevered, of course, maybe we'd have had those glimpses all over again. Dr Millikan might have been right. But we'd never know.)

There is no shame in divorce itself; what's more shameful is the circus around it. Court cases. Custody disputes. Counsellors who a lot of the time don't know what the fuck they're doing and have no conception of the damage they cause by giving their clients hope when there isn't any. The person being dumped doesn't see it at the time but it can be an opportunity for improving yourself and, the cliché of clichés, *growing*. For the unhappy party to merely give up on their happiness and stick with a broken relationship is arguably more of a betrayal. I was coming around to even approving of what Lara had done. In learning to survive on my own all over again, she'd saved my life, not destroyed it.

* * *

SMALL WORLD

'You fucking idiot,' said Giancarlo, sliding a three-quarter strong flat white under my nose at Piazzolla. 'I saw Olivia. You showed me her picture. What the *fuck,* dude? You make promises to her, go halfway across the world, sleep in her bed and tell her you're in love with *Frankie*? The woman's Glenn Close. Am I missing something here or are you just a fucking idiot?'

'Well, when you put it like that.'

'You could have put down a thousand dollars for a high-class escort, got the fuck of your life and you still would have been $4000 up on where you are now. Which is nowhere, by the way.'

'I didn't know I was still in love with Frankie until I got there.'

'In *love*? I'm just a wog from southern Italy but Fink, you're quite thick, aren't you? Look at me. I'm going to make it plain. *SHE. DOESN'T. WANT. YOU.*'

'Mate, I didn't want Olivia to come to Australia, give up her flat, her career, her friends, everything she had, when I'd be thinking about someone else. I already feel like enough of a jerk for what happened. Sure, I could have gone through with it. Yes, it was prick behaviour but I'm not a total prick.'

'I agree. But you are an idiot.'

'Thank you.'

'No. *Thank you.* That'll be $3.50.'

I might have been significantly poorer for my American trip, and I was as disappointed as anyone I was back at Piazzolla unloading my problems on a cynical Calabrian barista rather than helping Olivia tape up packing boxes in her apartment in Cambridge, but I was being true to myself. A bomb wasn't going to detonate if I didn't jump into another relationship. I had time to make the right choice. So many people give themselves over to someone who's not right thinking they might miss out altogether if they don't. Fear as much as love can drive relationships.

Which is why I felt so empowered having walked away from Olivia. I had conquered a fear. I was coming to appreciate the pleasures of being alone. The way I was feeling at that point, if I wasn't able to be with Frankie I didn't really want to be with anyone. Even Lara.

Yet I still craved physical intimacy. I wasn't totally 'with it'. When I fucked women I felt I was achieving something that I couldn't get from work or fatherhood or fitness. Rather than getting validation from just being myself I was still largely pegging my value as a man on the women I slept with and I was becoming more demanding of the quality of those sexual experiences.

Traditional dating no longer did it for me. The rub 'n' tug in Sydney during the break-up with Frankie, the time I'd spent at the Foxy stuffing dollar bills in strippers' G-strings and Giancarlo's throwaway comment about escorts had turned me on to something else I was amazed I hadn't seriously thought about before: paying for it.

CHAPTER 9

WHORING BY DEGREES

TRACK 9 'Hot Legs', Rod Stewart, *Foot Loose & Fancy Free* (1977)

Karina, or whatever she was calling herself that particular week, was a breathtaking vision straight off the plane from Buenos Aires; she wouldn't have been out of place at one of Silvio Berlusconi's *bunga bunga* orgies. Dark eyes. Full lips. A pair of impressive 'cans', as one infamous magazine boss of mine liked to describe that part of the female anatomy, on a tight, tanned, toned body. She hardly spoke a word of English but it didn't really matter as I only had 30 minutes on the clock and wasn't about to faff about telling her what I knew about Evita, tango and the 1986 World Cup.

Kissing was $50 extra. No anal. No *completo*. I went for the no-frills option – straight fucking with a covered blowjob

– yet when she went down on me or rode me cowgirl I barely felt anything. Not because of the condom. Rather because it was mechanical. Awful. Rushed. Devoid of emotion. I came out of the brothel feeling cheapened, ripped off and disgusted with myself for having surrendered to temptation.

It didn't last long. In a few days I was back. And a few days after that. Looking for the perfect hooker was just as fun as hunting for first editions in garage sales or combing through stacks of LPs at a flea market. I went all around Sydney visiting knocking shops and rub 'n' tug joints from high class to low, asking to see the girls rostered on, who'd chirpily parade for me in a succession of waiting rooms with the standard furnishings of an oversized plasma TV permanently tuned to sport and a coffee table laden with stacks of dog-eared lads' magazines. Like men think about nothing else but football and fucking.

'Hi, my name is Rochelle. How can I please you today?'

'Well, hello handsome, my name is Misty. I do a full service. Kissing, anal.'

'Pleased to meet you. I'm Shakira. How was your day today? If you have any questions, please don't hesitate to ask.'

I'd go to the front desk and tell the madams – invariably cigarette-ruined old crones – what I was looking for, which was essentially the kind of girl it was impossible to meet at bars or the beach without them being attached to some pumped-up, drug-dealing Lebanese homunculus. I wasn't after conversation.

'I'm after a pretty girl, hot, size 6 to 8, DDs or Es.'

It was tantamount to ordering Lara Stone. These were establishments not exactly oversupplied with beauties.

Brothel websites were misleading. Photos were either fake or airbrushed to the point of being unrecognisable from the girls who appeared in front of me. Or the sexy ones who were supposed to be working hadn't turned up, were sick or had broken up with their boyfriends. The excuses were endless. Instead you were invited to take your pick of the horrors they'd assembled in their place. A cast of shuffling grotesques straight out of Brassaï's Paris.

I usually opted to leave almost the moment I walked in. But occasionally I chanced on someone extraordinary.

Like Rebel, a young Kiwi art student with long tresses of flower-child blonde hair who was beautiful, smart and sensual. The kind of sweet, earthy girl you'd meet at an undergraduate house party and go on to marry and knock up. She fucked me so tenderly it was like she was my girlfriend.

Or Terri, a tall teen brunette with a pixie cut and a coathanger frame who gave me inordinate pleasure just lying down and spooning her. (I missed just having someone to hold.) I ended up partying with her, the madam and the rest of the rostered-on hookers at a brothel in Potts Point. In the harsh light of the kitchen, knocking back beers, cadging cigarettes and telling me about her panel-beater boyfriend, Terri was just a normal girl from the suburbs. But in the low light of her boudoir she was every bit the New York supermodel.

Yet there were also unsettling encounters. One girl, a platinum blonde, had looked alright in the parade and had a pair of extraordinary F-cup fake breasts that were only accentuated by her tiny body, but in the middle of our fucking I was overcome by the thought she might have once been a man.

I'm sure it was the OCD, but something about her just didn't seem right. She was too plastic. Her pussy felt too tight. She was too caked in make-up and when I looked closely at her she wasn't anywhere near as attractive as I'd thought she was. But her voice was like a female's. Her shoulders and waist seemed to be in womanly alignment. She didn't have a prominent Adam's apple. It was suitably Eve-like. Yet what could I say? 'Excuse me while I pull out for a moment, but did you used to be a *bloke*?'

I didn't know whether to evacuate or ejaculate. I ended up throwing caution to the wind, exploding inside her and fleeing as soon as I could. I hardly slept that night. It was scant consolation but I comforted myself in the knowledge that if she had once been a man, she was technically a woman now and identified herself as such. I hadn't crossed the orientation Rubicon.

I got to see other clients as I was spirited into anterooms on arrival or when I left by the front door. They weren't hideously fat or ugly. They were just normal young guys. Men like me who would have had no problem attracting women but for whatever reason were happy to spend hundreds of dollars not having to go through the torturous pantomime of dating. They were getting a guaranteed lay and, in many cases, saving money. (I'd been on one terrible date where a woman insisted on eating at an upmarket French restaurant, ordered three courses and a bottle of expensive Burgundy off the menu, then at the end told me she didn't fancy me at all, got up and left me with the bill.)

Inevitably there were also married men in among the brothel creepers, and men in committed monogamous relationships. I didn't agree with what they were doing. For all of my sexual adventuring, I still believed in fidelity – or at the very least in couples being open with each other about their desire to fuck other people. But when I went back to see Xanthe, the erotic masseur I had visited in that fateful 24 hours after breaking up with Frankie the first time, she explained to me that most of her customers were husbands who didn't regard what they were doing as cheating. They wanted to keep their families intact. They loved their wives.

They'd just lost the desire to fuck them or their wives didn't want to fuck them back. More or less the same issues that had wrecked my parents' marriage back in 1979. Monogamy was nice in theory but seemingly too hard in the real world. These men came to her to reignite the libidos that had coughed and spluttered to a halt after years of running on empty.

Xanthe told me she'd service a particular couple once a week and had done so for years. They'd take baths together, drink champagne and then she'd watch on, masturbating or dildoing herself, as husband and wife went for it on the massage table. She said they felt having her in the room heightened the desire they had for each other and took their own sex to another level of pleasure.

I'd visit brothels and discover there were people I knew who had double lives. During one line-up at an upmarket place in Sydney's east, Nadia, a girl I'd been flirting with for some time on Facebook, a leggy Belarusian who worked for a car rental firm and had the same eyes and lips as Charlize Theron, walked in wearing lingerie and didn't let on when she recognised me. She just continued her spiel and then tottered out of the room on her high heels.

When I got home I emailed her and told her I had no issue with her being a prostitute. She emailed back, saying she didn't know what I was talking about. But a few hours later she emailed again and invited me out for a drink.

When we met in Potts Point Nadia confessed she'd been a hooker for years. The brothel was in fact a side gig. Normally she worked as a $1000-an-hour escort for a private agency but business was slow. She told me she was a manic depressive and had a lot of pent-up energy. Fucking – and getting paid for it – was the best way she'd come up with of coping mentally without medication and maintaining a lavish lifestyle that was otherwise unsustainable on her regular salary.

We caught a taxi to BBQ King in the city for a 2am feast of Peking duck and ended the night at a dubious Asian 'health' spa kicking back in white bathrobes on adjoining La-Z-Boy recliners and sipping Chivas Regal while two elderly Chinese men kneaded and pounded our feet. It was one of the most bizarre nights of my life. To relax, Nadia often came to the same place for some 'Korean': getting her pussy eaten by one of the female masseurs.

'Oh, and before you ask, I won't sleep with you,' she said, swirling the ice in her tumbler.

'Er, okay. I'm curious. Why?'

'You just don't do it for me, Jess.'

I turned up another time to a terrace in Glebe for a private 'tantric' rub 'n' tug (whatever that is) and was greeted at the door by Sabine, a glamorous and busty Tahitian. She almost fainted when she saw me. We'd originally met at my mate Arnon's bar when a friend of hers, a German woman

I'd met online but who'd just been deported back to Berlin for overstaying her visa, asked her to make me a proposal. Would I consider marrying the German woman for cash? I politely declined and instead we'd ended up making out in front of the bemused bartender.

For this reason she wouldn't go through with the booking. She'd already felt bad enough kissing me behind her friend's back. So she took me out to lunch, where she explained that although she worked as a fashion stylist for some big magazines and had a good career, jobs had dried up recently and erotic massage was the only way she could afford the things she wanted: label clothing, eating out at good restaurants, overseas holidays. A lot of her friends in fashion were doing it on the side, too. I'd met some of them previously and not suspected a thing.

By committing that mistake with Frankie, I'd been exposed to a whole new seam of the city I'd lived in all my life, a seam that exists in every city around the world: the dark underbelly of illicit sex. We lie about it. We keep secrets about it. But it's there and it's thriving. From what I saw, there was nothing sinister about it; nothing to have to hide away and be ashamed about.

Everyone was whoring. There were the paid whores I was visiting. The unpaid whores I met prowling bars for rich men and living in their bikinis by swimming pools and on yachts.

The once brave actors selling their souls to Hollywood to appear in brainless cartoon shit and collect big pay cheques. The talented directors shooting tampon commercials so they could continue sending their kids to private schools. The earnest politicians betraying their values and beliefs so they could get ahead inside the machinery of government.

And yet as a society we have the nerve to look down on sex workers. They were strikingly normal when I sometimes passed them on the street or in a supermarket aisle and we exchanged silent but knowing looks. Our derision should be reserved for those who try to pretend that what they're doing is any different.

* * *

I met Patricia, the age-indeterminate (but I guessed early 40s) widow of one of Australia's most powerful men, via a dating site. She was frequently talked about in the press and to some degree the attention bothered her but in person she was no different to any other woman I'd ever met. Sensitive. Vulnerable. Emotional. Except for the fact that she lived in a waterside palace, was invited to all the fancy parties and would never have to work a day in her life.

Patricia had an incredible body and knew how to fuck. Her marriage had been an open and swinging affair. She told me some incredible stories. Orgies with prime ministers and captains of industry. How one renowned billionaire, long married, a giant of the international corporate world, had wanted in on the couple's private sex parties but was told he was too old and turned away. Paying off Italian police for having cocaine stashed on their private plane. Wild romps in foreign cities that would go on for weeks with groups of prostitutes. And her late husband, a flabby old rooter, was a pillar of society. He'd had a state funeral, paid for by taxpayers.

At the time Patricia was fucking me she was also fucking a well-known Australian sports star being passed off in the press as a loyal and dutiful partner to his dowdy girlfriend. He'd turn up drunk on Patricia's porch in the wee hours of the morning huffing and puffing like the big bad wolf to let him inside so he could bang her brains out. But Patricia had no problem turning him away. She had her hands full with plenty of other men. She fucked tradesmen. She took young lovers. She'd just come out of a torrid affair with a visiting Canadian athlete. There was a lot of humping going on in her house but not a lot of loving.

I suggested she might have a sex addiction. Funny, coming from me.

'God, you think?'

'When you fuck a 20-year-old who comes to sand your floors, yeah, I think there's a distinct possibility. You should talk to someone.'

'Who?'

'A shrink.'

'No, I couldn't.'

'Why not? *Do it*. What have you got to lose?'

Patricia went ahead and made an appointment with a psychiatrist. A week went by. I came over for another midnight tryst. We were lying naked in her bed, with its mountain range of pillows and debenture of expensive Egyptian cotton sheets and bed linen, watching *Dexter*.

'So how'd it go with the psych?' I said, turning to her on my pillow.

'Well, I told him everything. Then he fucked me.'

Despite my urgings, Patricia wouldn't report him. She feared what the press would do if the story got out. She said she'd already been put through the wringer enough after her husband's death. Which just goes to show that given an opportunity with the right woman, even those men who take the Hippocratic Oath will try to get their ends in.

Patricia wanted to be held until she fell asleep and didn't like waking up on her own in the morning. She got upset when I put my clothes back on and said I wanted to go home. She even raised the idea of a relationship with me, almost as unreal a scenario as the two of us hooking up in the first place. We were chalk and cheese, with clashing attitudes, wildly divergent means and from different worlds. But in bed none of that mattered.

Meeting Patricia, I realised it was all bullshit. Many people we hold up as models of social respectability are frauds. Supposedly conservative couples are in fact swinging polyamorists. What does marriage mean anymore when so many people are afraid of the idea of it, those already married are often breaking up on increasingly spurious pretexts or taking lovers or going to prostitutes or massage parlours, while countless others are torturing themselves in silence or whacking off to internet porn?

Others stay married for the money, too afraid to lose their 'security'. Then there are those poor people with religious upbringings who can't countenance the idea of breaking up their marriages for the shame it would heap on their conservative parents or their 'community'. The essence of marriage is commitment but what are we committed to? Mutual happiness or just living together come hell or high water even when one or both of us are miserable?

* * *

'You don't change, Fink. You're still a fucking idiot.' Giancarlo was just warming up. 'America, *again*? Do you ever learn? They won't let you in the country after the last time. Olivia will have reported you to the Department of Homeland Security. The call will have gone out: turn away at border.'

I flipped the laptop screen around and showed him a picture of Sunny, my latest object of desire. She'd told me she was a part-time legal clerk when we'd started talking but there was no way a girl that hot, at 36, was working in an office doing the photocopying. She then admitted she did some stripping and eventually, after a bit of prompting, she revealed she was an escort.

'Is it still worth going, Giancarlo?'

'Sorry. I was wrong. You absolutely *must* go.' He looked again. 'Holy *shit*.'

Sunny was the kind of girl who appeared in Whitesnake videos. Wild mane. Rock-hard fake tits. Tiny waist. Face like a cheerleader. An All-American heart attack. She'd been photographed by the great erotic lensman Earl Miller, was a Penthouse Pet, had appeared on the covers of a stack of porn magazines and was now happily working in the San Francisco Bay Area under the name Savannah. I'd written to her on an American dating website and slowly, over a period of months, we'd fallen for each other.

I hadn't really cared when she'd disclosed her secret; in fact it had fascinated me.

For five years she'd flown to Las Vegas each weekend to dance at the famous strip club Crazy Horse Too, where patrons were regularly beaten up by the owners for non-payment of bills. When her shifts finished she'd gamble and hustle at the Hard Rock. She'd worked as a private dancer for a businessman from Georgia. He'd spent half a million dollars just to look at her – no sex – before he squandered his fortune on the stockmarket and she squandered hers on coke and designer clothes and partying hard with LA rockstars.

Which accounted for her battle with the bottle. She now had a kid, an angel-faced three-year-old daughter, and was in the middle of a divorce from a supposedly straight-up guy she'd met while stripping who'd promised her a lot and not come through when it mattered. He had his own addiction problems. But she assured me she was sober and was looking for love. I was so entranced by the prospect of my own *Pretty Woman* fantasy playing out that the unsavoury fact she was getting fucked by strangers several times a day was a minor detail, a tolerable inconvenience. I did my best to shut it out of my mind. We agreed to have a holiday together and see what happened. She wasn't averse to the idea (mine) of making adult movies as a boyfriend–girlfriend team, like the pornstar Kelly Madison and her graphic-designer husband, Ryan. They were raking it in and I'd had a gutful of writing about sport. I hadn't been an expert before I became SBS's top sports columnist. I didn't see any reason why I couldn't make a similar go of it in porn. But Sunny preferred to keep turning tricks. She enjoyed it. She was making an unbelievable amount of money, 50 times more in an hour than what she could make in a regular job. Taking home in two days what I'd be lucky to make in two months.

'Get into male escorting, babe,' she urged me. 'You'd *kill* it.'

In a tough and sometimes dangerous business she'd kept a healthy sense of humour.

* * *

Every couple of hours I'd get a photo of Sunny sent from her phone, each one of ever-increasing sexiness. On all fours on the floor in front of a mirror. In the shower, her tits lathered up with soap. Dressed in lingerie in her hotel room waiting for clients to arrive or the cops to bust down the door. (Having a number of gentleman callers visit her room frequently aroused the suspicion of other guests.)

Sunny had the most amazing body I'd ever seen, one arm completely covered in tattoos. It was hard to believe

WHORING BY DEGREES

I was talking to a real person and not a cover illustration from *Heavy Metal* magazine. We'd talk on the phone and masturbate while talking to each other.

'Are you coming?'

'I'm gonna blow a hole in the ceiling.'

'I want you inside me.'

'I'm inside you, baby.'

'I want you inside my pussy. My pussy is so wet.'

And so on.

When she picked me up in her litter-strewn SUV at San Francisco International Airport – her jet-black hair pulled back in a ponytail, big red '70s-style sunglasses on her nose, a tight white cotton tanktop showing off the assets that had emptied the bank account of a self-made man from Atlanta – Sunny mercifully kept both hands on the wheel and away from my penis. I'd surely have lost it to a head-on collision otherwise. Her idea of driving was being a moving traffic violation. Rather than talk as we flew down the Bayshore Freeway she cranked up Eagles' 'Already Gone' and lit a cigarette. She looked over at me and smiled. I wound down the window and felt the wind in my hair. This was better than my hackneyed Norman Rockwell vision. This was California. This was freedom. *This* was 'the life'.

It was hardly surprising in retrospect, but it quickly emerged that beyond our shared love for vintage clothes and Bad Company we didn't have much to talk about. Sunny was a high-school dropout from Sonoma County whose peerless body meant she hadn't had to work so hard on her education to get ahead. She couldn't spell. She cared very little for books, art, politics or world affairs. But she didn't need to. Whatever our differences, I was still there to fuck. As Giancarlo had said, there was really no question I should come to America, even if was just for the sex. Unlike the previous time with Olivia, there was no pressure about any decisions that had to be made. We were just two people making something out of the time we still had on earth. Having fun and forgetting the exes and the custody arrangements and the attendant cavalcade of stress that comes when relationships break down.

I hadn't been with a woman so completely in charge of her senses erotically. She fucked for money but she was fucking me for what we both hoped could be love. Feeling the immense heft of her tits pressed against my palms when she went on top and the slapping of her butt cheeks against my body when I fucked her from behind, I'd arrived at a point of sexual nirvana I never thought possible, even after everything I'd experienced with Lara, Marguerite and Xanthe, the erotic masseur. Being a romantic hopeless case/undiagnosed sex addict wasn't so bad when I ended up in situations like this one. Far from what I knew, upstairs in a beautiful apartment in San Francisco, filling the suprasternal notch of a Penthouse Pet with come while the distant hubbub of Chinatown slipped in through the half-closed windowpane.

Sunny had told me before I left Australia that she wouldn't work while I was there, yet just minutes after we'd fucked on my third or fourth morning in San Francisco, lying back on her big old four-poster bed, her mobile phone rang.

'Can I get this?' she said.

'Sure.'

She took the call. 'Hello, Savannah speaking,' she said. 'Yes, this is me. Yes. Why thank you. Oh, *thank you*. You're too kind. This afternoon? I can do 2pm. Where? Santa Clara? *Uh-huh*. Yes, I have a car. Text me the address please. Yes. To this number. I'll see you then. And what's your name again, baby? *Wayne*. See you soon, Wayne.'

Of all the bizarre situations I'd been in since breaking up with Lara, this was one I hadn't mentally prepared for.

'*Savannah*? Sunny, I thought you said you weren't going to work.'

'Babe, I've been losing a lot of money since you got here.'

'Yeah, but Sunny …'

'Come with me to Santa Clara. You can go sit in a café. It's only for an hour.'

'While you fuck someone else?'

'It's not fucking, Jesse. It's *work*.'

As much as I had been telling myself that I was cool with the idea of Sunny taking money for sex, the reality of what she did hit me then. From afar her profession had struck me as glamorous and exciting, but in reality it was banal. The ease by which she could switch from making passionate love to me to flirting with some hard-up nerd from Silicon Valley on the phone unsettled me. I didn't want to sit in a café and wait for her. I hadn't come all this way to be her pimp.

She made herself up, went to her booking and I stayed in bed. Whatever we'd had during those four days together was extinguished then and there. Another disconnection.

Only long afterwards would she admit she didn't believe in love.

'I don't believe in traditional relationships, Jesse,' she told me in an email. 'They all disappoint and fail in the long run with terrible pain someone is left to deal with. People aren't built to be with one person. If I could find a man that was okay with my work – and that's the only thing it is – then I would consider having a relationship. I just prefer to spend all my time making money. That's my pleasure.'

Clearly, she wasn't alone.

* * *

WHORING BY DEGREES

Before flying back to Sydney I went down to LA for a week and stayed in Beverly Hills with Taylor, my online friend who'd broken up with the Australian soap star. With a fridge full of kelp and a small dog that was about to commit suicide from boredom, she wasn't my type at all, and I wasn't hers. Friendship was good. One afternoon she drove me out to Venice Beach to buy a pair of Moscot sunglasses. We parked the car and went for a walk down Abbot Kinney Boulevard. An hour later we returned to the car and were about to get in when she nudged me.

'Look up,' she said. 'Across the street.'

I looked up. There was a guy standing on his balcony in a faded orange T-shirt and dark sunglasses, smoking a cigarette. He was looking across at me. I was looking straight at him.

It was Robert Downey Jr.

Luck. Fate. Chaos. Sliding doors. The music of chance. Whatever it was that had brought me there at that moment, I was grateful. Photographing him with my phone would have spoiled it. I smiled and got in the car.

CHAPTER 10

THE BUCK'S NIGHT

TRACK 10 'Buckets of Rain', Bob Dylan, *Blood on the Tracks* (1975)

When did it get so hard? Why has finding love become so complicated? When I first saw Lara, halfway through 1996, seduction techniques originated and later perfected by generations of cavemen were deemed totally acceptable. We were at a rock gig in a church hall in Stanmore, in Sydney's inner west. People were milling about talking and drinking between sets. Lara was with her on-again, off-again boyfriend Hugo, a greasy-tressed Balmain musician who would go on to have a national hit and make millions but at the time was a penniless bum who lived by the credo 'what happens on tour, stays on tour'.

Up till then, I was just 23, Lara 25, I hadn't laid eyes on anyone so lovely. Just the sight of her made me nervous.

THE BUCK'S NIGHT

I wasn't so experienced with women. I'd lost my virginity when I was 19 (late for this day and age), had had no more than one or two girlfriends and half a dozen one-night stands, and went through three years of university fancying myself as Johnny Depp in *Don Juan DeMarco* but having all of the pulling power of Fogell in *Superbad*. The most outrageous thing I'd done to that point was have sex for three days with the 22-year-old daughter of my mother's nudist boyfriend who was also the half-sister to my half-brother. Figure that out.

When I tried to pick up Mia Freedman, who went on to edit Australian *Cosmopolitan*, in one of our journalism lectures she turned around to me in her seat and hissed, 'My boyfriend's in Florence', like there was nothing else that needed to be said. *In Florence.* Girls like her were out of my league and they made me know it.

But I'd felt I'd learned from all my rejections and was never going to die wondering. I decided that Hugo, a dismal but magnetic slob of a man who slept with groupies every other weekend, didn't deserve any more chances with Lara. So I walked up to where this beautiful girl was standing, began chatting to someone nearby, and pressed my back against hers to let her know I liked her. I didn't know any better. That innocuous encounter, hardly romantic, would result in Lara and Hugo breaking up for good and segue into a ten-year relationship: the longest of either of our lives.

Now, in my mid-30s, divorced from Lara, a single father, a far more sophisticated, accomplished and well-rounded man than when I was 23, I was meeting more women than ever before but singularly incapable of having a relationship that lasted more than a few months, and that was if I got lucky. More typically I'd meet someone and be informed by my 5'2" date that at 5'9" I was too short to be considered a serious candidate for anything other than picking up the drinks tab.

Heightists like these are growing in number. You see them everywhere on dating sites. Assuring you they're not superficial, spelling out their desire for a man of substance, someone who's self-made and who's good to their family but then adding the all-important rider: 'Gentlemen, if you are under 177cm, please don't contact me.' Women given licence by their beauty, demand and the bounty of the internet to pick and discard males like they're sorting through fruit at the supermarket. Doing to men, of course, what we've been doing to women all these years. There's a hell of a lot of payback going on.

Had meeting Lara in such an innocent, clumsy way been a rare privilege of my youth? Did young people still meet like that? Probably. But I couldn't walk into a rock gig at a church hall now and do that to a woman. I'd be arrested for indecent assault. I was feeling my age acutely: prevented from reviving the social life I'd enjoyed in my early 20s by a mash-up of inescapable realities and commitments that come with parenthood and simply growing up. Just like everyone else who's loved and lost and found themselves suddenly single when they're least prepared for it. I couldn't get into a hot tub time machine and go back to when it was easy. I wished I could.

The internet, a vast lacuna of disconnections, might not be perfect for finding love, for it commodifies something that cannot be broken down into a nutritional information box just like anything else on a supermarket shelf, but the alternative for a lot of us is stark. It keeps us thinking we're connected. And that's far better than realising we're all alone.

*   *   *

That Lara and I lasted so long was remarkable, really.

For a start, we broke up after two weeks, when my future wife decided things were getting too serious too quickly and she needed time to 'heal' after Hugo. I was beside myself. I couldn't sleep, eat or do anything. I took to standing outside her pokey Stanmore flat in the rain, like John Cusack casing Catherine Zeta-Jones in *High Fidelity*, looking for any sign of her or the new man I expected her to be with behind the timber shutters. It really could have gone either way – including a stalking charge. But after a campaign of earnest letter writing and horrible poetry, back in the days when people actually put pen to paper, stuffed that paper into an envelope, bought a stamp for it and put it in a postbox, Lara came back and gave me a chance. Had it been 2012, of course, I wouldn't have seen her again. She'd have put her picture on a dating site, married a Texas oil billionaire and blocked me on Facebook.

Then there was the fact that our interests were totally mismatched. She'd read one book in the decade prior to us meeting – and that was a biography of Keith Richards. I had an apartment crammed with books ranging from first editions of French erotica such as *Les Aventures du Roi Pausole* to vintage manuals on rose pruning. (It really would have been easier for everybody if I'd ended up a gay man.) When we went to the cinema she'd fall asleep before the last reel. Every time. It drove me batty because I still consider one of the great pleasures of going to the movies to be that short walk of a few hundred metres back to the car from the cinema doors, discussing what you've just seen. I never got to have that talk with Lara. She had very little curiosity about the world. Her geography was dreadful. She could have easily run off with someone far more suited to her – one of the members of the Australian band Powderfinger was pursuing her hard – but for whatever reason she chose to stick with me.

THE BUCK'S NIGHT

Last of all, our relationship had flowered in less than auspicious circumstances. An orgy. Lara had ditched Hugo and we'd been dating for about two months when we decided to throw a dinner party. A few friends came over to my place, including a well-known Australian actor. We all got riotously drunk, as was our habit at the time, and an impromptu spa bath with me was suddenly raided by the rest of the partygoers, including the actor, who had eyes for Lara. As all men did at that time.

I quickly realised, like Jerry Seinfeld, that I wasn't an 'orgy guy' – the sight of the actor attempting to get hot and heavy with my girlfriend made me deeply uncomfortable rather than excited – so instead of joining in I went outside and played ping-pong with Hamish, a longtime friend who'd similarly declined to be involved, not on the grounds of revulsion but because of his impending wedding to his English girlfriend. We played about a dozen matches listening to the low moans coming from inside the house.

Eventually, hours later, some sheepish and remorseful figures emerged from the spa, thanked me for my hospitality and the curry I'd cooked and went home. Lara crawled into my bed. The next morning, while she was sleeping off the night before, I cleaned the clogged pubes out of the filter of the spa bath. The things we do for love.

* * *

In those early years Lara and I fought a lot. Many times we were dangerous to be around. She threw a right hook at me in the face, connecting fully, when a girl asked me to dance at a party. She did it again, this time with an open hand, when one of her friends threw her panties at me in a karaoke bar and I jokingly sniffed them. Another time at another party she asked the famous Australian actor Richard Roxburgh to sign her bum. He kept his dignity. I was absolutely furious and was very close to walking out on her.

But Lara enriched my life because of our differences. Putting aside her looks, sex appeal and impetuosity, she was still a good and kind person. We shared an intense sexual attraction and our personalities somehow meshed. A man can offer a woman many things, but unless they share chemistry, what is the point? We had chemistry. Ultimately our relationship wouldn't survive, of course, but while the going was good it was passionate, fulfilling and happy. A veritable wellspring of Stephen Vizinczey's 'glimpses'.

It was love.

We became engaged not long after the orgy. Paradoxically, the spa drama had brought us closer together, while many of the others involved split apart, some longstanding friendships fracturing for good. Lara asked me to marry her one Sunday morning while we were lying in our bed. But we didn't rush into marriage. There were no rings, we stayed engaged for

THE BUCK'S NIGHT

18 months and we used the time to work through all our jealousies and insecurities and figure out if we were really right for each other. When the moment came to get married, we knew: we were ready. She trusted me and I trusted her.

So I wasn't going to jeopardise it all with a buck's night, a bone-stupid tradition I absolutely detested, but which a small group of school friends insisted on hosting for me a week before the wedding.

'I don't want one.'

'You're having one.'

'No.'

'Come on, you fucktard. It's happening, whether you want one or not. It's not all just about you, Fink.'

I relented and asked them to organise a poker game. Something quiet that would pass off without a hitch. Especially not something that involved a naked woman in any way, shape or form. That would invite catastrophe.

The game took place at a friend's apartment. It was suitably muted but blokey enough with cigars and whisky to keep everyone pleased, all very Neil Simon-ish. But after an hour it went pear shaped. There was a knock on the door and a stripper walked in with her male bodyguard. She looked like a butch lesbian: a bottle blonde with short spiky hair, flabby, rough as guts. She shoved me to the floor and I went along with what she was doing because I didn't want to upset my friends and ruin the evening for them. But looking back I shouldn't have been concerned with what they thought. In the course of doing her dance routine with a boombox, a cigarette lighter and a can of shaving cream the stripper tore the underwear I was wearing right off – in half, like a sheet of paper – and left deep red scratches on my chest. I was mortified and angry but there was no point getting into a fight with my friends, who were just as embarrassed and shellshocked as I was. In fact, two of them had been so frightened by the she-beast violating me they'd hidden in the kitchen. They couldn't bring themselves to look. When I got home and tried to slip into bed unnoticed, Lara realised something was awry, as I feared she would. She got to her feet and accused me of sleeping with another woman. Hugo's infidelity had scarred her deeply.

'You fucking arsehole. I fucking *knew* this would happen!'

'Lara, really, it's not what you think.'

'I can't believe you'd do this to me!'

'I haven't done *anything*! I didn't want a fucking stripper. I wanted to play cards. They organised it, the fucking idiots. I had no idea she'd turn up. I went along with it. You've got to believe me. She was horrible, if it makes any difference.'

'Then why are you wearing someone else's underpants? They're two sizes too big.'

'I had to borrow them. She tore mine in two.'

THE BUCK'S NIGHT

'You've got scratches all over you.'

'Uh, I know. I don't know how I got them.'

'You fucked her! How could you, Jesse? You fucking arsehole. I fucking hate you!'

Lara was getting hysterical now. She was crying. Losing it. Totally.

'I didn't fuck *anyone*! I didn't do *anything*!'

'It's off. It's fucking *OFF*! You're a piece of *shit*. I can't believe it. Get *OUT*, Jesse! *GET OUT*! Get the fuck *OUT*! *GET OUT! GET OUT! GET OUT!*'

She was shaking violently. Her head looked like it was about to burst.

What do you do with a hysterical woman? You slap her, don't you, to make her snap out of it? I distinctly remember picturing that scene in *Airplane* where the lady is having the panic attack in her seat. There was a queue of passengers lining up to slap her, including a nun and a Hare Krishna. It was one of the funniest scenes in the movie. But this wasn't funny. It was taking place in front of me. Real life.

Lara froze and clutched at her face.

She began sobbing and fell to her knees on the bed. I reached down and pulled her head into the crook of my shoulder.

'I'm sorry, baby. I'm sorry, I'm sorry, I'm sorry. I love you. I *LOVE* you!'

LAID BARE

* * *

The next day Lara forgave me when I had a chance to properly explain what had happened with the stripper and we'd both calmed down. We made love. She said she loved me and she was sorry. She felt terrible. But it wasn't as terrible as I was feeling. She was now sporting a very faint bruise near her left eye. A week before we were going to gather in front of hundreds of our friends and family and get married.

Lara reassured me she'd put make-up on it and no one would be any the wiser on her hen's night that evening at a Korean bathhouse.

But the make-up ran away in the steam. Her friends saw the bruise and Lara, rather than fabricating a story, told them what had happened. To some of them, the mitigating circumstances weren't relevant. I was a pig. To others who knew the details, including my family, it was just an unfortunate mistake brought about by too much emotion and too little communication. My mother was particularly angry that Lara had let it out. They all wanted us to move on.

Our wedding day arrived and Lara looked more beautiful than I'd ever seen her before. We sang 'Reminiscing' together at the reception with a band made up of Sydney's best jazz musicians, her friends. We had a romantic honeymoon in the Indian Himalayas, saw a tiger in the jungle and came home early to buy our house in the Blue Mountains: our first home. Everything was perfect.

But the trauma of the buck's night, and that bruise, sent me to another place. Up until that point in my life – I was 25 – I'd not known any kind of emotional or mental problem. I'd been normal and happy. That's how innocuously life-changing mental illnesses can start. For months after the wedding I received emails from people overseas telling me they'd heard all sorts of stories on the grapevine. Most were wildly inaccurate. No matter if I told them what really happened at the poker game and afterwards or how much Lara reassured them we were happy and moving on, they had made up their minds. They didn't want to know me anymore.

In the wash-up I'd go on to lose half a dozen friends, some of whom I'd known since primary school. Most I never saw or spoke to again. One told me he'd regretted 'letting you in my life'. Another pretended she didn't know me when I passed her in the street. (She still does to this day.) A third, the best female friend I had, would come to me years later after Lara and I had broken up and apologise for having shut me out. She'd made contact, she said, on her therapist's urging so she could let go of the guilt she felt.

But it was too late for me.

From that point I changed. I felt no self-worth. I had no desire to exercise, to see people, to go to parties, to talk on the phone or even visit my family. I felt listless and unmotivated at work. I was as close to Lara as I had ever been but now I became more reliant on her. She became my conduit to the outside world. I began retreating inside myself and starting to obsess over other mistakes I'd made in my life. I even managed to fear I'd raped a girl while she and I had been very drunk when I was 19, only the second time I'd had sex. Had her consent been valid? I went back to her through her family and asked, receiving assurances that everything was okay, not to worry and to 'get on with your life'. I even paid a criminal lawyer to check the *Crimes Act* and give me the all-clear. But I couldn't stop worrying. Despite intense efforts to overcome the worry, I obsessed about it for 12 hours a day, every day, for three years.

I wasn't aware of it then, but I was succumbing to Horace's 'black dog' and the utter hell of OCD.

* * *

Three slow, pitiless years.

Me falling deeper into despair and struggling to work to my capacity, function socially and keep my head above water in my marriage; Lara doing what she could to connect to the man she'd married and not the dead weight I'd become. But the man I used to be was now well and truly gone. I had

THE BUCK'S NIGHT

ballooned physically, from my normal weight of 72kg to a touch over 100kg. I was desperately unhappy. I was someone else now. And it had all started from one mistake. Just like the one made by the character Harry in *The Slap*, the Christos Tsiolkas novel and subsequent ABC-TV dramatisation, and as calamitous to me, my family and the lives of others as Harry's had been in Tsiolkas's book. One mistake can change a life. (Years later, one rainy winter afternoon at Piazzolla, I'd meet the man who played Harry in the TV series, the Australian actor Alex Dimitriades, and tell him and everyone at Piazzolla my story. They were supportive and sympathetic but more than anything stunned that what Alex had just put to screen was not far removed from what I had gone through myself.)

When I wasn't morose, I made lists in my head. Endless lists that sought to solve whatever mental riddle I'd set for myself that day about problems I had that really weren't problems. If I didn't find an answer, usually obtained through hours of searching on Google, I wouldn't be able to meet friends for coffee, go to dinners, even sleep. I felt incapable of doing anything physical. The meditative quality of running, once something I'd sought out, terrified me. It was just an invitation to dwell on whatever was plaguing me.

The lack of information about the illness also compounded my alienation. There seemed to be only one shrink in Sydney who even knew what Pure-O was – and that was because he had OCD himself. The expert in the field, Dr Steven Phillipson, was based in New York. He'd given the illness a name. There was no self-help group I knew of in Sydney, or anywhere else in Australia. There were few books specifically about the subject, and I ordered all of them from Amazon.

But the best resource was the internet, where Dr Phillipson published his excellent papers and chat rooms such as Stuck in a Doorway offered a chance to talk to other people suffering like I was.

There was little understanding from my family, either, even though one of my relatives had also been diagnosed with OCD. His would manifest itself in endless rituals of checking and counting. Some mornings it took him hours just to get out of his room. My father didn't want to accept that I had the disorder and thought it could be solved with naturopathy. My mother, by contrast, pushed whatever SSRI she had in her bedside drawer into my hand. My wife suggested acupuncture. I tried all these suggested remedies but none worked.

Lara and I needed a circuit-breaker. So we decided to take a holiday in France and try to have a baby. On our first night in Paris, in a dark hotel room in the Marais, she got pregnant. It was magical. The first time we'd tried and the best sex we'd ever had because we were in love and we wanted something better than the dish of shit that life had served up for both of us since the wedding. We came home renewed and optimistic. There were no complications with the pregnancy and the birth, despite a scare when Evie got some fluid on her lungs and fears she might have a hole in the heart, was similarly smooth.

But OCD didn't want me to be happy. I was having intrusive thoughts even in the delivery room. What should have been the most joyful moment of my life was a reservoir of pain. If there were any doubts I had this malevolent anxiety disorder, they were quashed when my psychologist's diagnosis was confirmed by Professor Gordon Parker at the Black Dog Institute in Sydney, Australia's top depression clinic.

One night at home I began watching a documentary on SBS about child rape in South Africa. It was so disturbing I had to turn it off after 20 minutes.

It unconsciously stayed with me. While I was changing Evie's nappy the next morning, standing over her, the involuntary image of an erect cock flashed before my eyes. It was over in half a second but the way it crippled me and changed the course of my life, it might as well have been a bullet to the head.

CHAPTER 11

LIFE'S FURNITURE

TRACK 11 'Mandolin Rain', Bruce Hornsby and the Range, *The Way It Is* (1986)

So Lara and I weren't dealing just with the arrival of our child – a challenge for any relationship in those first few years of infancy – but the fact that my mind was being ripped up every day by the most repugnant OCD thoughts possible. The more I tried to avoid what I feared thinking, the more the thoughts would come. The most minor chores and activities became a minefield of anxieties.

There didn't seem to be any way out. There is, which is acceptance that everyone gets bad or jarring thoughts, OCD afflicted or not. You need to refuse to take emotional responsibility for those thoughts and keep yourself fit, strong and focused in mind and body, but it would take me years of struggle and hard work without drugs to get to that point of self-actualisation. It would help, too, to discover that some of my acquaintances and close friends, half a dozen in fact, men I never thought for a minute harboured any kind of internal torment, shared similar symptoms and anxious fears.

One confessed he had the impulse to jump off buildings. Another had the urge to swerve his car into oncoming traffic on the Harbour Bridge. Another had similar sexual obsessions to mine. All were struggling in silence, trying to shut out their pain through the usual trinity of park football, casual sex and hard drinking. They felt as much relief as I did to be able to talk to someone openly and without the fear of being misunderstood. But they wouldn't have ever talked about their anguish unless I had brought up mine in the first place.

The collateral damage of my OCD was my marriage to Lara and my subsequent relationship with Frankie. I loved both women and I lost them because I was in a scary place at a time of my life when I couldn't give them all of me. I also pushed them away because my love for them and my fear of losing them was interpreted as control. It made me sad that they couldn't see the person I managed to become. The person my ex-wife fell out of love with was bookended by two other people: the person I was when I brushed up against her back in that church hall and the person I am today. When I look at photos of myself from that period when I bottomed out, I don't even recognise myself. There is an unsettling disconnect, a sense of disbelief. Like Jason Bourne being told his real name is David Webb.

The one constant in my life was Evie. She was my rock. I didn't have to try to impress her or look good for her or reinvent myself for her. She loved me for who I was. She was always quick to respond with 'I'm not going to talk about it' when I asked for an update on Lara's relationship status. She was happy to be dragged to cafés and draw in her sketchbook while I read the newspaper. To be introduced to my eccentric girlfriends. To eat cooked-tuna sushi every night of the week because I didn't want to clean up from cooking. To find money under the bed so I could go buy a coffee at Piazzolla. To go on torch patrol when our flat got hit by bed bugs. To go to my mother's for a sleepover when I wanted to be with a woman. To be parked on the couch watching endless reruns of American tweeny pap on Nickelodeon while I surfed dating sites to alleviate my loneliness and boredom. I concede that my caregiving during much of this time could have been better. Evie covered my arse.

When I first arrived in Darlinghurst she'd been a little pink Ewok. She'd go walking with me through the streets of Kings Cross, past the fat strip-club bouncers and drug-fried tramps, in her fairy wings. She'd do elaborate dance routines on street corners to songs she'd sing out loud – ABBA, Boney M, Rolling Stones – and didn't care if people were watching. She wasn't scared to talk to people or order things she wanted from cafés or newsagent counters and pay with the coins she'd collected in her sparkly Chinese junk-shop purse. She loaded up calico shopping bags with blank pads and textas when we went out to restaurants and had no interest in the electronic gadgets other kids wasted their time on. What made her happiest was going out for frozen yoghurt. She even passed on the sugary toppings in solidarity with my trying to lose weight.

She was growing up before my eyes. With her symmetrical features, flame-coloured locks and impish nature, she'd been spotted by a talent agent who'd seen her out with me and went on to front a couple of advertising print campaigns. Lara and I had no problem with her being in front of the camera – indeed my ex-wife, turning up for one audition, had also been picked up by the same agent – and thought it would be good for her character and to put away some money for her future. When she started being teased at school about the ads she was in, however, she unilaterally called an end to her first foray as a budding movie star. I didn't mind. Turning up to casting calls and seeing the way kids were being pushed and cajoled into doing something they didn't want to do by tragic stage mothers living vicariously through their prettier offspring left me angry. It was up to her if she ever wanted to go back. She had the intelligence and awareness to make her own decisions.

On occasion I was chided for my 'cool dad' style of parenting. When Alby, now 65, came over one morning and saw I'd left my bed unmade but was asking Evie to make hers, he snapped that I was going to turn her on to 'sex and drugs when she was 16'. I was so livid I physically muscled him out of the front door and told him to go fuck himself. I was particularly ashamed about that after everything he'd done for me; his comment being just a clumsy way of telling me to lead by example. My reaction was inexcusable.

I was frequently in the wrong. I still made mistakes. I was nowhere near perfect. But Evie was always there, by my side. An independent, self-styled, self-assured, street-smart, cluey kid who'd charm anyone she met.

Even when I caught a plane to somewhere in the world, her only caveat was that I not die.

'HI DADDY,' she scrawled on a note to me before one such trip. 'I LOVE YOU VERY MUCH. THE ICE CREME WAS NICE BECAUSE IT WAS CHOCLAT FLAFER. HOPE THE PLANE DOSEN'T CRASH BECAUSE IT'S TO ELEY FOR YOU TO DEYI. AND I NEDE A DADDY. ♥ LOVE EVIE.'

LIFE'S FURNITURE

* * *

You see it on dating websites everywhere: 'No baggage.' But I was happy to have mine. I was left with nothing from my divorce but a small cheque from the sale of the house in the Blue Mountains, a few photographs, my books and my clothes. Lara even claimed my banjo. When Frankie left, she would go on to take the only thing of material value in my house, the painting of Evie, and for months afterwards came to collect the other small ones she'd forgotten about. I was cleaned out both times.

Being on the losing end of two significant love affairs had left me with life's furniture: the emotions, experiences, memories and lessons that come with throwing yourself at the mercy of love. I was rich in those possessions. I didn't need a flash car, a busty nail technician on my arm or gold on my body as totems of my masculinity and virility. I felt I was more of a man because I'd dared to take the risk of lifelong commitment: to a woman and to a child. I had been deficient. I'd made mistakes. I'd copped a beating in the spin cycle of OCD, a divorce and a failed relationship. But I was a better man coming out than I was going in. Even with a couple of loaded bags by my feet.

* * *

Why, then, when I'd managed to get on with my life post Lara and Frankie and slay the OCD with exercise, eating well and confronting my thoughts head-on did my mother say what she did?

'Oh, by the way,' she casually mentioned one day while I was visiting, 'Lara thinks you look hot.'

It was an innocuous comment, made with no ulterior motive, and Sal, I think, had said it just to make me feel good. I *hoped* she had. This was a woman who had tried to set up Lara with one of my best friends, Gully, a recently separated firefighter and father of two young boys, while I was still trying to get back with her. I'd put that down to my mother's eccentricity rather than malice. Gully and Lara had both been appalled. When I confronted her about it and asked her what the hell she was thinking, Sal offered a typically baroque defence: 'Well, you two were never going to get back together. I thought it would make them both happy.'

But with that casual comment my finely calibrated recovery campaign was thrown completely off balance.

For four years Lara had rejected all my approaches, turning me away like a border guard would a refugee without the right papers. Every time she'd tell me, 'I need to be on my own', 'I just want to be friends', 'This is not the right time' or 'I'm working on myself'. There was never even the remotest hint of willingness to try to reconcile and put our family back together. That was a dream I'd given up on long ago.

Now she thought I was *hot*?

Your ex-wife is not supposed to find you hot, no matter what you look like. She's supposed to find you loathsome and repugnant or just be emotionally neutral about you. It's easier to process her rejection of you that way. Finding you even partly attractive is an ember of possibility you don't want when you've finally managed to get your shit together and 'move on'.

'Huh?' I replied, astonished. 'When did she say that?'

'She came over for dinner last night.'

'What happened with David?'

'They broke up.'

Another ding in my recovery. More than a ding. It was now a write-off.

'You know, son, if you listened to me just once I could help you. You need to be her friend. Nothing more than her friend.'

'I can't be her friend.'

'Then you're a stupid fool.'

'I was her husband. The father of her child. I don't want to be her fucking *friend*.'

'Be her friend. Be her friend for five years if you have to. That's how long it might take if you ever want to get back with her. Don't even think of trying to sleep with her.'

'Five *years*? What? And stand by like an idiot while she fucks other men?'

'Your problem, son, is you never listen. And I can't help you if you never listen. Forget it, then. Forget I ever mentioned it. Forget all about it.'

* * *

It was too late for that.

I sent Lara a text telling her I'd heard what had happened with David. We spoke on the phone when I rang Evie. She called me a few times just to say hi. I gave her my blessing to use money Evie had earned from a modelling job to buy an air ticket to Bali and have a holiday with our daughter. Oddly, she even sent me a text message to wish me a Happy Valentine's Day. At first she revealed very little about the break-up with David but eventually she opened up more than she ever had before and I was mindful not to come across at any point as gloating or having told her so. The polar ice cap between us was thawing.

It had only taken four years for her to figure out David was far worse than I'd ever been and to compound matters she'd gone and bought a house with him.

Lara told me David was an emotional cripple. He was a ponytailed fuck-up who cared more for home brewing and watching the footy than he did love and – her word – she 'hated' him.

Clearly, it was all very new. So new that he was still coming over to her place to walk Bosco, the grandson of my first dog, Bogarde.

'Why the fuck is he walking our dog?'

'He loves that dog. More than he ever loved me. He's good to him.'

'Hang on. I love that dog. He's *my* dog. He's living with you because I live in a cupboard and you have a house.'

'It doesn't matter. Jesus. I don't have time to walk him. Let it rest. I don't want to talk about it anymore. I'm exhausted. I need time for me.'

My mother's advice was ringing in my ear. *Be her friend.*

'Come out for dinner with me and Evie.'

'Why?'

'Just dinner. It'd be good for Evie.'

'Well, I have been thinking we should do that for her.'

'I'm not going to try anything.'

'So long as that's all it is. I really don't have the energy for anything else. I mean it, Jesse. I'm so tired of it all. I'm sick of men. You're all fucked in the head.'

* * *

Lara and I went to dinner with Evie at Caffe Tozzi, an all-night Italian restaurant in Kings Cross. I was apprehensive: could I do it, could I be her 'friend'? I should have listened to my gut and pulled out, but I went with my heart and it was one of the biggest mistakes of my life. After so many years apart it was a weird feeling being together with my family, my Norman Rockwell vision. No relatives or friends to be human shields. Ricardo, the owner of the restaurant and a friend, came up to me at one point and whispered in my ear: 'Your wife, she's *beautiful.*'

I was so nervous about the occasion I drank a bottle of red wine even before Lara and Evie arrived at my flat. When Lara ordered another bottle while we were at dinner and then told me she'd only have a couple of glasses because she was driving, I stupidly drank the rest. I thought I could handle it. I couldn't.

I raised the issue of David at the table. It was like the elephant in the room. Lara reacted and the mood of rapprochement suddenly turned hostile. She asked for the bill. When we had walked to the junction where the famous Coca-Cola sign stands at the corner of William Street and Darlinghurst Road, I tried to give Lara a hug and a kiss. She pushed me off like I was an overgrown spider attacking her. It was a scene. In my shiraz reverie I'd intended for her and Evie to stay the night at my place. Instead she was running the few hundred metres back to the car with our child to get away from me.

'You haven't changed, you're still the same,' she said, putting Evie in the car.

'And you're still a selfish bitch,' I shot back, like the fool I was. 'It's all about you, Lara. It's always been just about you. "I need time for *me*. I need this. I need that." You fucked our family. Pissed away our family for that *cunt*. And for what? I'm supposed to have sympathy for you? Give *you* time? While all that time you wouldn't have pissed on me if I was on fire.'

'Evie, put on your belt.'

'Don't go,' I said, putting my hand on the driver's-side window.

'Let *go*!' Lara shrieked, pushing away my hand and rolling up the window. 'Go back inside or I'm going to call the *police*.' That word again. Evie was now crying. 'Look at what you've done, you're scaring our child. Fuck off, Jesse!'

'You fuck off! Don't you fucking go!'

Lara had reversed her car out of the driveway and was now in the laneway. I was standing in front of it, my hands down on the bonnet. Neighbours' lights had been turned on. There were people looking at us from their windows.

'Move, or I call the police.'

I knew that very moment there was no hope for us, no way back. Even worse, I'd upset Evie and showed her the anger I thought I'd dealt with long ago. I'd ruined the whole night by getting drunk and mentioning David, but why had I chosen to give Lara so much power in the first place? Why had I agreed to her conditions? Why, after four long years of rehabilitation and reinvention, was I seeking her approval and not the other way around? I wasn't the pitiful fraction of a man I'd been when she'd left me. I'd turned my life around and prevailed, even prospered. I was an idiot for letting her walk all over me in the divorce and I was doing it again. Rather than controlling her, she was controlling me.

I stepped aside and let her pass. She and Norman Rockwell could go to hell.

* * *

Not long afterwards, I found out through Evie that Lara was in a new relationship. She'd hooked up with an old friend, Wes, a surfer and actor from her high school days in Wollongong. He still lived down south. My daughter assured me he was a nice guy, 'much nicer than David'. I had ceased to care anymore. 'I need time for me' and 'I need to be alone' had meant nothing. The fact was that Lara didn't want me. But I was happy for her. I cared enough about her happiness and my daughter's happiness for both of them to have a decent man in their lives. David hadn't been anywhere near that. In my eyes, having come between Lara, Evie and me at a time when I believed our family could have been saved, he was beneath contempt.

'So how's Bosco?' I asked Evie. 'I haven't seen him for ages. We should get him to come over for the school holidays.'

'Mum gave him away.'

'What are you talking about? To who?'

'To David.'

I couldn't believe it. Lara hadn't even thought to ask me. She explained she didn't have time for Bosco anymore because of her new relationship with Wes and all the driving she now had to do between Sydney and Wollongong. Our dog, the only link to my beloved first pet, was living with the man who had choked me and left me unconscious in a garden bed.

The guy stole my wife. Now he was stealing my *dog*? My life was turning into a John Irving novel.

I briefly considered asking her to get Bosco back and finding a new place with a yard so I could take him. Lara, mortified at how I'd taken the news, offered to try to get him back. Kirk, a Piazzolla regular who prided himself on his machismo, seriously proposed we kidnap him.

'No, I couldn't. It'd just cause more problems than it's worth.'

'Fuck that cunt. Let's put some expanding foam in the tailpipe of his Hillman.'

'No.'

'Mashed prawns behind the door panels? In the air vents? C'mon, Fink. The smell will never go away.'

'I appreciate the offer, dude. But leave it.'

Like I had so many times, with Lara, with Frankie, the only choice was staring me in the face.

I had to just let it go.

* * *

Some time later I had a date with a woman called Lindy. Not unlike Lara: busty, vivacious, a head turner. A magazine publisher, she was the mother of two kids, had recently separated from her wealthy husband and was going through that early stage of not being sure whether to try to repair her marriage or just get on with it and start a new life. She ended up walking out. I'd told her all about my story, from the buck's night to the choke to the divorce to Frankie to my adventures with women of the night to my escapes overseas to losing Bosco.

We were in a bar in Potts Point and after showing me a picture of her kids on her iPhone she got a notification on Facebook.

'This guy keeps on poking me,' she said. 'A muso. Won't leave me alone. I met him at a wedding. He's a friend of my sister.' She paused. She was looking intently at the screen. 'Fuck. *No*. Surely not.'

'What?'

'No, it can't be.'

'What are you talking about?'

'You won't believe it. Oh my god.'

She handed me the phone. I took one look at his full name and his profile picture and sprang across the room like I'd seen a snake.

It was David. Was I the butt of some elaborate cosmic joke? Would this cur ever fuck off out of my life? When was enough *enough*?

'What should I say to him? I don't want to be his friend after what you told me.'

I thought about it long and hard. There were so many ways we could have gone with it. I kept it simple. I couldn't help but laugh. What else was there to do? This really was a John Irving novel.

'Just say, "How's Bosco?"'

CHAPTER 12

ALL PLAYED OUT

TRACK 12 'Cold as Ice', Foreigner,
Foreigner (1977)

Where there's beauty there's complication. Like a rune passed down from Odin himself, this aphorism is implicitly understood by men entering the battlefield of love and is supposed to guard them from unnecessary pain brought about by heartache, anxiety, despair and maxed-out credit cards. But in the presence of beauty the minds of even the most intelligent, secure and stoic of men turn to mush. Women have long known this, of course, and taken full advantage of their looks to get what they want.

There are the usual gold-digging beauties, like Patricia. They choose a soft target – loners who've inherited family fortunes or superannuated tycoons married to gargoyles from Jim Henson's Creature Shop – and go for it. As long as they can stomach the sex, it's easy pickings.

Then there are the beauties who are garden-variety nut jobs, like my serial runaway bride Chloe. Typically they're 'creative' or 'spiritual' types or a combination of the two: actors, models, painters, sculptors, writers, bloggers, journalists, singers, photographers, stylists, make-up artists, fashion designers, graphic designers, yoginis, Pilates teachers or vintage-clothing peddlers. Women long ago liberated by their physical attributes and commensurate sex appeal to be utterly bonkers and with whom it is completely impossible to have a relationship. They always have boyfriends or a long line of male suitors and thousands of Facebook friends, no matter how selfish or sociopathic their behaviour, and for them madness is not a curse but a carefully cultivated indulgence.

I'd met and been fatally attracted to a number of them since my divorce. There was the well-known Australian actress with tremendous knockers who phoned me one night to instruct me to 'just go outside, look at the moon, then call me back' only to fail to pick up the phone when I did as I was told. She was one of the sexiest women I'd ever met but completely barking insane. Or the tall blonde restaurateur who shagged me, invited me over to her place for dinner the next night and then concocted a ridiculous story about being the mistress not just of Australian billionaire James Packer but his late father, Kerry. When I picked holes in her story and it was obvious she was just making it up as she went along, she asked me to leave before we'd even had dessert. Which I did, gladly. I feared I was going to be stabbed with a fork.

But now online dating and social networking has made women even more aware of their value and spawned the rise of a third kind of 'man trap': female players.

It's no longer enough for an attractive girl to meet a man at a bar or a friend's barbecue or a rock gig, think he's handsome and nice and take a chance on a relationship. The internet encourages the checklist mentality to go feral. Men under 5'10" might as well jump off a bridge and be done with it.

Where once women could be the object of bounded lust at their local surf club, shopping mall or school fete by dint of their sex appeal they can now be minor web celebrities simply by uploading some alluring photos on Facebook.

The friend requests pile up. The invitations pour in. Soon enough they get added to nightclub door lists, attract followers on Twitter (despite having nothing interesting to say) and start appearing in the social pages, head thrown back, Hermès tote on one arm, hand to hip with the other, contorted in a so-called 'skinny arm' or 'akimbo' pose. Some are signed up by publicists. Others become bikini designers. Virtually all of them end up married to rich men. They never have to pay for food, drinks or party drugs again. But where a male player's primary motive is to use women for sex, a female player typically seeks different temporal pleasures that can range from being fawned over to being showered with gifts, to having everything paid for, to being granted a hall pass to the easy life for ever after. They also have good sex with handsome men for fun – as man-eaters have always done.

They'll forget your name at parties – even the ones you've snogged in the dark corner of a nightclub when they thought you were somebody important. They'll be more interested in checking their text messages than anything you ever have to say to their faces. They'll be as emotionally giving as a Mesopotamian relief at the British Museum. They'll sadistically toy with you, just like the half-dozen suckers they're sadistically toying with at the same time and which you're unaware even exist.

No matter the indignities these women heap upon you and the lack of satisfaction they bring to your life beyond their anatomical symmetry and the occasional half-hearted blowjob, you keep coming back for more punishment like the gormless simpleton you are.

Because all men, fundamentally, are idiots. Women are going to play you with the sweet raggedness of a bluegrass fiddle.

I know all this from hard-earned experience because I am the idiot king. Not only would I get played by one of these women but it would happen when I was trying to play her. The player would be outplayed.

And in the process I'd lose not just one woman – but two.

* * *

'Oh my god, Jesse. You look like just like Robert Downey Jr!'

Though it still amused me, it was something I was getting used to hearing. But this time it was different. I wasn't hearing it from a stranger. I was hearing it from a girl I'd yearned for but hadn't seen or heard of in 25 years, Keira.

An English girl who'd tormented me at high school, she'd been my unrequited crush when I was 13. I'd written her love letters and dreadful poems inspired by or directly plagiarised from the 1987 Steve Martin movie *Roxanne*: 'I am in orbit around you. I am suspended weightless over you like the blue man in the Chagall, hanging over you in a delirious kiss.' I'd even stolen a photo of her draped on a horse from one of her friends' tackboards at a party and kept it in a shoebox for near-three decades. After throwing away so many of my things after the divorce, including wedding photos, I still had it.

Keira was the girl every teenage boy lusts after. Posh. Tanned. Blonde. Ridiculously pretty. Long legs. Swimmer's shoulders. She hadn't given me the time of day in 1986. I hadn't looked anything like Robert Downey Jr back then.

ALL PLAYED OUT

With my round glasses and pimple-flecked chin, I'd looked like Adrian Mole. While she dated older boys in rock bands, I drew penises in Tintin books at the school library. There were so many cocks in *Cigars of the Pharoah* it eventually had to be taken off the shelf and withdrawn from lending.

Now it was 2011. She'd just joined Facebook, was living in her mother's beachside guesthouse in Greece and finally, after quarter of a century, she'd noticed me.

* * *

She was 37, and now a brunette, but from the pictures I saw still very much the Keira I remembered. Her looks weren't a concern. What was a concern were the photo albums of movie stars such as Brad Pitt and Tom Hanks, dolphins, the royal wedding of Prince William and Kate Middleton, and the Victoria's Secret model Miranda Kerr. It struck me as the handiwork of a bored juvenile. Keira *was* bored. She hadn't worked for a couple of years since breaking up with her Greek bar-owner boyfriend and was stuck in an existential rut, not knowing what to do with her life.

She got by with an allowance from her rich father, and insisted she wanted to be independent and earn her own money but was wedded to the privileged lifestyle into which she'd been born. Lazy days on the beach. Pimm's in the afternoon. Luxury goods. Prada bags. French perfumes. Skiing holidays at the best resorts in Switzerland.

Looking back now, all these things should have been red flags to keep away from her. I could barely afford a round of sushi for my kid. And it wasn't like I hadn't warned myself not to fall for another girl on the internet. I'd had too many disconnections there.

This, however, was Keira. My teenage fantasy girl. I felt I knew her and trusted her, even though we'd never actually said a word to each other in person beyond a 'hello' in the high school quadrangle in 1986. The real truth, the one I didn't want to acknowledge, was that I didn't know her from a bar of soap. But that didn't stop us falling in love through our computers. Fool's love. The love of adrenalin, yearning, fantasy and make-believe. Not real love. I knew what that was from Lara and Frankie and it wasn't this.

Yet I would ignore the warnings of Alby, Sal, Giancarlo, Enrico, Kristin, Ron and the beggar with the wheelchair on the corner of Hughes and Macleay to tread warily and chose to invite Keira to come to Australia and move in with me, sight unseen. I'd had enough of being alone. I wanted to take another risk, even if it meant having to stare down the OCD that engulfed me when I formed an attachment to anything. I believed if Keira and I could fall in love it would be the perfect denouement to my romantic career. The full circle.

ALL PLAYED OUT

My first crush would become my last wife. This Peter Sellers would get his Britt Ekland.

Hamish, my ping-pong partner from the orgy, had been at high school with both of us and, just like the rest of the male student body, had nursed a crush on Keira. Even though he'd been married to the same woman since his early 20s, was living in London and had a family of his own, he admitted the prospect of my hooking up with her stuck in his craw 25 years later.

'Yes, dammit, I'm jealous. But you can't make a decision about having a relationship without seeing her, you jammy tosspot,' he said. 'Get your arse over to Europe and have a fucking great summer making love to her while you decide.'

I ignored that advice too. The situation was too romantic for caution. We'd both made up our minds. Keira had had enough of hanging out with the wandering peacocks in her garden and told me she was coming back to Australia. She just had to book her ticket and sort out her affairs in Greece and her visa with the Australian embassy in London. Something that should have been resolved within a couple of weeks but, because of her reluctance to press her father for more money, would end up dragging out over a period of three or four months. Towards the end I didn't know whether she was really coming or not.

Which opened the door to Phoebe entering my life.

LAID BARE

* * *

I couldn't quite believe this white-blonde leg factory deigned to even talk to me. She was around my height and didn't demand that I be 6'2" just because she was beautiful, with long tanned pins that went to the sky, and could have had her pick of any man. She was not even 30 and I was at the wrong end of my 30s. She kept herself immaculately groomed and dressed in designer clothes while I rarely shaved and cobbled together outfits from whatever I could find at the Wayside Chapel op-shop.

Girls like her weren't supposed to go out with guys like me, especially when I had nothing to give her but eternal gratitude.

But we had the regulation drink, I went to kiss her and she kissed me back. No gong sounded. I wasn't informed that I was being filmed for *Candid Camera*. She kissed me again. Softly.

'That was lovely, thank you,' she said, getting into a cab. 'Call me, Jesse Fink.'

Phoebe was in the social pages. She worked for a fashion house. Her sister dated a movie star and was hiring herself out as a no-sex 'companion' to an eastern suburbs businessman for random dinners and weekends. Just to be seen with him. There were a lot of women like that in Sydney.

ALL PLAYED OUT

Phoebe assured me she wasn't one of them. She was a normal girl who'd just arrived from Melbourne and didn't go in for all that showiness. She hated the superficiality of Sydney. Her sister and her sister's friends were trying to get her to sign up for a promotional modelling outfit that was effectively doubling as an escort agency. She wouldn't bite.

Wherever she went she turned heads. It was an empowering feeling walking beside her. Not so much from the ego boost but the social cachet. People respond to you better when you have a beautiful woman beside you, from ordering drinks in a bar to running into people you haven't seen for a long time. They look at you differently. They smile. Slap your shoulder. Take a keener-than-usual interest in what you're doing. Life becomes easier. You're no longer the shifty-looking hopeless case everybody thought you were. You score chicks like *her*? You're an enigmatic, redoubtable *genius*. What a joke.

But what I liked more about Phoebe was that I could just be with her at home after making love in the late afternoon and she'd be more comfortable in one of my tatty old T-shirts than her expensive lingerie. Which, in my eyes, made her even sexier. Not every man wants to see a girl blow hundreds of dollars on lacy smalls at a boutique when they can get as much pleasure in seeing her in something oversized or even misshapen they own. It's a guy thing. But Phoebe would still spend an hour in the bathroom afterwards. I'd never met anyone so attentive to their appearance. I wasn't complaining.

Yet how could I get out of this catch-22? I wanted to commit to Phoebe but that would mean losing Keira, the object of my schoolboy fantasies. But to see Keira would mean losing Phoebe.

So, crazily, I tried to satisfy them both. I played the 'I'm just feeling you out' ruse with Phoebe while telling Keira I couldn't wait to see her. When Keira pulled out, as I expected she would, I'd go to Phoebe and tell her I'd made up my mind and she was everything I wanted.

Neither girl knew the other existed but my diabolical plan almost came unstuck when I embedded the Van Morrison song 'I'll Be Your Lover, Too' on Facebook and they both thought it was dedicated to them. Two big fat 'likes' right next to each other.

It was getting dangerous. I was leaning towards Phoebe but there was a glimmer of something about her that wasn't quite right. She'd only call me or return my calls late at night, sometimes at 1am. It was subsequently explained to me by a shrewd male friend that this meant I could never say, 'Where are you? Let's do something' and put her on the spot. Then when I finally got on to her she'd always schedule to meet on a Monday or Tuesday night, never a Friday or the weekend.

ALL PLAYED OUT

On those days she was invariably 'tired' from work or going out on the town with her sister.

So I held back. But the more we'd meet on those Mondays and Tuesdays the more my feelings for her developed and eventually I decided to walk up to Piazzolla in the late afternoon, as I always did, and explain to the Darlinghurst Council of Elders – Giancarlo, Enrico, plus the usual cast of artists, tradesmen, restaurateurs and retired criminals – my predicament. They'd seen Phoebe when she'd dropped in for a coffee with me. What should I do?

'What are you, fucking *mad*?' said Enrico, throwing his arms out in exasperation. 'What part of your tiny brain thinks chasing a woman you haven't seen for 25 years and asking her to move in with you is a good idea? That's stage 56. You haven't even got to stage 1. Call it off. Tell her not to come. Go out with the incredible fox you've got here. *Jesus.*'

He was right. I wasn't cut out for two-timing. I'd lost my mind. I resolved to tell Phoebe I wanted to be with her and tell Keira to stay in Greece.

But when I rang Phoebe and suggested we get together for dinner on the Friday, when I'd planned to put my heart on the line, she told me she couldn't see me the entire weekend. A 'friend' was up from Melbourne and she'd be showing him around.

On the Saturday her 'friend', a young man called Bryan, posted on Facebook that he was at the Three Sisters in the Blue Mountains with Phoebe and tagged her. It showed up on her page. Naturally, I checked his page. Bryan had a chiselled jaw. Designer stubble. Single. Wasn't a homosexual. He was 'interested in women'. There was no way he was a friend. I was furious and sent her some texts, admonishing her for her dishonesty. Phoebe said it wasn't what it seemed; she was looking forward to seeing me. Bryan, meanwhile, continued tagging her. On the Sunday she was with him at a nightclub in Sydney. On the Monday she posted that she'd received some red roses at work. By Tuesday she'd changed her relationship status.

It was a perfect storm of deceit.

That Phoebe had allowed her romantic grifting to be revealed to me on her Facebook wall was nasty. But that's how young people roll in the age of computer love. They're not just disconnected emotionally but to what counts as sensitivity. But I had grudging admiration for her. I thought I knew everything about women but hadn't counted on this. The scenario that I was being played hadn't even entered my mind. I'd done it hundreds of times before but never had it happen to me. And – this part would surprise me – it actually hurt.

* * *

ALL PLAYED OUT

When Keira announced she'd finally booked her ticket and was holding her working visa, good for five years, I wasn't going to lie to her about Phoebe. That's one of the good things for anyone in a relationship with someone with OCD. Honesty is a compulsion, so you'll always know what your partner's been doing behind your back.

Keira was great about it; she said she didn't blame me for feeling unsure about where we stood with each other when she hadn't made concrete plans and it was only natural that I had felt lonely and sought the company of another woman. She didn't even ask me for details. It was a reaction I hadn't expected.

Even though Keira and I had met again in unconventional circumstances I was genuinely convinced this time it was all going to work out. And I needed a lucky break. After four years with SBS's sport department, my critical editorials about the Australian soccer federation, the Australian World Cup bid and soccer's world body, FIFA, had landed me in trouble with senior management at the network, who wanted me to soften my tone and write less about politics and corruption if I wanted to continue in the job. Indeed, a complaint had allegedly been made about me by the federation to FIFA itself – an extraordinary turn of events that raised the ire of the soccer writers' association. Not coincidentally, SBS was negotiating World Cup TV rights. As a journalist and writer who'd gained some notoriety because of my refusal to bow to anybody, I thought the request was unconscionable.

I was SBS's most read sports columnist but that didn't stop them from following through on their threat and not offering me a new contract. A total mental breakdown, a terrible divorce and now, through no fault of my own, a profile I'd spent half a decade building shot down – it was quite the trifecta.

I wasn't going to let the fuckers have the satisfaction.

I hit back by going on national television with the ABC's flagship current affairs show *7.30* and accusing the network of ethical abuses, conflict of interest and editorial interference.

SBS, a publicly funded broadcaster with its own codes of practice, had for a long time pressured me and other opinion writers to stick to a pro-Australian World Cup bid line even when the bid was clearly a shambles, and censored what didn't fit 'preferred editorial policy'.

Many said I was mad. Others predicted my career was over. But I was taking a risk, sticking my neck out and being true to my principles. Sometimes you just have to say 'fuck it' and ride out the consequences. Even though SBS had offered me a meal ticket to a great life, a life without integrity is no life at all. It was the best piece of advice my father had ever given me and, like I had so many times before, I was following it.

But I'd lose a friendship in the process.

Will, the English producer who'd started 'HTO' with me all those years ago in that Hamburg nightclub, was now a big fish at SBS. He'd frequently warned me to be careful with my opinions but felt I'd betrayed our friendship by going to the ABC and revealing information that he said was given in confidence.

The decision to appear on *7.30* was one of the hardest of my life. Though I told the ABC I didn't want Will 'implicated in any way', the story couldn't go to air without some of that information being disclosed. The ABC wanted it to run. I was tormented and sought the advice of Alby, Sal, all my close friends and even Lara. My friendship with Will mattered to me more than he knew but there was something bigger at stake, a greater good: namely the editorial independence of a publicly funded broadcaster and maintaining the ability of all journalists at SBS to do their jobs without being pressured.

When both my parents told me to do what felt right, two people who never agreed on anything, I knew what I had to do. It was no accident that after the program went to air the only other SBS writer who dared to be interviewed to back up my claims, Davidde Corran, was told his contract wouldn't be renewed. He, like me, hasn't worked for them since.

Will stayed on with SBS. Davidde and I took a hit for sticking up for what we believed in.

But there was some comfort to be drawn in the idea that SBS as an organisation might be better for having been kicked in the arse. Certain people could go on flying business class to FIFA pow-wows in Zurich.

I'd kept my integrity.

* * *

I was now completely broke. From afar Keira didn't care. We had the romantic notion of cooking at home each night. We would sell clothes to make ends meet. We'd go into business together and import vintage sunglasses from America. Everything was going to be fine once she got to Sydney. She was optimistic and reassuring and she loved me. That was all, she said, I needed to think about. The rest would take care of itself. Together we could do anything.

When she arrived early one rainy winter morning we couldn't even get our kiss right. She got a cab in from the airport and had checked into a boutique hotel not far from where I lived. I gave her a couple of hours to settle in and then walked up to meet her, waiting outside with an umbrella on Darlinghurst Road.

ALL PLAYED OUT

When Keira came down the stairs to meet me, she said she wouldn't kiss in the street.

'There are people looking.'

'So what?'

'No, this is not how I pictured it.'

'What the hell are you talking about?'

'I wanted to meet you in a dark bar. I'd be waiting for you, drinking some red wine. You'd walk in. We'd see each across the room. You'd walk up and kiss me. I didn't want it to be like this.'

'Well, I'm here. That's what's important. Go with it.'

'This is not how I wanted it to be. I'm so disappointed. Why'd you want to meet *now*? It could have waited till tonight. I'm not ready for this.'

After 25 years apart and five months of longing to see me, hundreds of emails and countless Facebook pokes, she was arguing about *how* we should kiss, rather than just doing it and enjoying the fact we had finally come together.

From there my relationship with Keira – if I could call it that; we were strangers about to move in together – just got worse. Nothing was spontaneous. Everything I did was wrong. As I'd gleaned from the photo albums on her Facebook page, she had totally unrealistic ideas about how life should be, all conjured from the movies. She couldn't deal with reality. Walking through the streets of Darlinghurst, the streets

I loved, she'd almost jump to the side when we passed a junkie, muttering to herself that 'Life's not romantic, I'm seeing that now, it's just hard, *hard*', as if being with me in Sydney and not Notting Hill or the south of France was some sort of purgatory.

I tried dragging her to the gym so we could work out together but she'd complain after 20 minutes of half-hearted cycling on an exercise bike. When we went shopping at the supermarket, I'd want to get in and out as quickly as possible. She'd spend half an hour smelling laundry detergent, unscrewing the lids and sniffing the contents, trying to find just the right one.

I desperately wanted to get the glimpse of eternity I'd been hoping for but it just wouldn't come. I had never felt more distant from a woman. Yet again it became clear to me what the internet can sometimes do: create a totally false reality where two people can fall in love, live their lives remotely and think they're happy. But unplugging from that parallel world and finding a connection that actually counts for anything face to face is something else altogether. Why couldn't I learn?

I broke it off with Keira after six weeks when she told me excitedly she was going to a department store in the city because 'it's the only chance I'll ever get to see Miranda Kerr'.

ALL PLAYED OUT

I looked at her, all of her 37 years, expecting a punchline. It didn't come. She was serious.

And then it dawned on me what had been the problem all along: the girl I had fallen in love with at 13 was still 13.

* * *

It took four weeks for Keira to move out. I wasn't even there when she got her things together and called a taxi. We agreed it was for the best. And it was. She ended up taking to life in Sydney, getting a job with an upmarket jeweller and finding a flat in Darling Point. It was a big deal for her to be on her own and earning her own money. I was proud of her, as was her family back home. She knew nobody but she wasn't short of suitors or marriage proposals from men she'd meet randomly in bars or shopping malls. They showed her a side of the city that I couldn't on my income but she consistently rebuffed their advances. She wanted to be alone and not fall back into her old habit of relying on men.

Two months after our break-up I dropped off some mail to her at her shop one evening. We ended up having a drink and going down to a beach by the harbour at midnight to wade ankle deep in the shallows. There was phosphorescence in the water, something I'd never seen. Keira kicked the water gleefully like a child on holiday. I was so taken away with her beauty that I kissed her. A lapse. But something had changed. For the first time in my life she was no longer an unrequited crush, a ghost of the past, a face in my computer or the woman I was supposed to marry. I was finally getting to know who she really was: a true innocent. And even though we weren't meant to be, I loved her for that.

* * *

I'd made a gross error of judgment holding back on Phoebe. I'd fucked up. Yes, I'd been played, but being the idiot king I'd given her permission to play me. Women aren't stupid. When a guy says, 'I'm really happy getting to know you' that means he is or is planning to sleep with other women. I said it to Phoebe and it was a permission slip for her to start collecting other 'potentials'.

Phoebe confessed as much when I went to see her at her boutique in Paddington. I went on the pretext of returning a silver chain of hers I'd found under my bed but all I wanted was to see her face again. Not on Facebook or in the memory card of my phone. Face to face. Like real people.

'I'm sorry, Phoebe. I made a mistake.'

We were standing by the counter in the middle of the shop entrance. There were Saturday customers milling about around us, checking the price tags and eavesdropping.

'It is what it is, Jesse. You know I adored you.'

'And I adored you. I was just in a totally impossible situation. I couldn't not see Keira after all that time. I wanted to *see* her. I wanted to *be* with you. I didn't know what to do.'

'I know. I sensed it.'

'Fuck. I feel like such a fucking idiot. I shouldn't have let you go.'

'If it's any consolation I don't know what I want anymore. Bryan is a great guy but, oh god, he's so *full on*. There's too much pressure. He wants to marry me. I've only been seeing him for two months.'

'I want you to know I wouldn't marry you.'

'I know you wouldn't. Maybe that's half the problem.'

I smiled. 'Does he want kids?'

'Yes. And I want kids. But I'm not ready for that. Not now anyway.'

'Come out with me.'

'That's *sweet*. But I've got two other men who are romancing me. I have my hands full right now with that and work.'

'Come on. Just a coffee. As friends. Please.'

She shot me a pained look. 'Okay, *okay*. But not this week.'

I kissed her on the cheek and left the shop, a spring in my step as I walked back to my car. I'd lost Phoebe once. There was no way in hell I was going to do it again.

But she never returned my calls. I found later she'd dumped Bryan and taken up with another guy she'd already known for some time.

It appeared she'd been playing both of us.

* * *

Why do men seek out beautiful women when they cause so much heartache? My original falling into player life came from not being connected to women largely because I was still in love with my wife. It was never a calculated decision of mine to be a man whore, much less hurt anyone. But until I met Phoebe I wasn't at all aware of what it felt like to be on the other end of the playing equation. The one getting burned off. I felt violated. And I never wanted to do that to any woman again, even if it meant giving up the chance of easy casual sex.

There's a theory that the more opportunistic women in the dating scene zone out from having feelings or showing empathy as a protective mechanism against being played themselves; a sort of emotional insurance against the inevitable hurt some men are going to dish out.

I don't buy it. Women can be apex predators too, just as adept and ruthless as any man. Some are even more calculating. They know what they want and they know how

ALL PLAYED OUT

easy it is to get, especially online. Men on the receiving end can complain of exploitation by this new robot army of well-groomed sociopaths in six-inch stilettos but these women aren't exactly reinventing the wheel. More worrying is the fact that fools like me go on dating them because we have access to them through the click of a button.

CHAPTER 13

INTO THE UNKNOWN

TRACK 13 'Landed', Ben Folds, *Songs for Silverman* (2005)

We are in the twilight of novelty, living in a mash-up culture with no new riffs, no new stories, nowhere to go that's new. Our sense of awe at human milestones has been replaced by a sense of awe at James Cameron movies. We have instant access to just about everyone and everything yet love remains elusive for most of us. It should have become just another commodity to be packaged and sold as a $1.99 app but it stays unharnessable and unbreachable. It's what makes it a precious prize and why it remains so.

I met Sir Edmund Hillary once, in a Sydney hotel room five years before he passed away, aged 88, from a heart attack. The great mountaineer and explorer was in town for a dinner put on by his charity, the Himalayan Trust, to celebrate the 50th anniversary of the 1953 British summit expedition and I'd scored an exclusive interview with him thanks to my friendship with the Tenzing Norgay family. Years before I had done a book with them and they'd given me a rug from Darjeeling. They were wonderful, humble people. 'Sir Ed' hardly did any press so this was the proverbial opportunity of a lifetime for a young writer.

Hillary was chatty, humorous and gave me much more time than his second wife, June, was happy to give me. His first, Louise, had died in a plane crash with their daughter, Belinda, in 1975. June grumbled to herself in the background as Hillary ignored her reminders that we were over time and fully emptied his memory bank answering my questions. He was still whimsical about what he and Tenzing had done, half a century after the event.

'I think we were the lucky ones, quite frankly,' he told me. 'We had the whole mountain before us. That was the time to really be there – when it hadn't been trampled all over by literally hundreds of people ... if you go through life and feel like you've done everything you've wanted to do, well that sounds like a pretty dull life to me.'

For anyone, meeting one of the great explorers of history is an experience you remember for the rest of your days.

I was no different, though I left the meeting feeling more inadequate than buzzed.

Why?

The most profound effect Hillary had had on me for that hour and for a long time afterwards was that he'd made me confront myself. He'd conquered his unknown.

What was my mine?

* * *

After my divorce and losing Lara, I felt my personal frontier was love and it was online dating that could offer the adventure my life had lacked. Despite its inherent faults and pitfalls, there's a fantastic randomness to hooking up on the net. One drink and a glint in an eye can turn into a night of erotic adventure. Anything can happen. You can meet anyone. You can end up anywhere. It's chaotic and addictive as well as compellingly incestuous: degrees of separation are ever shrinking because of social networking. Stanley Milgram's famous six doesn't apply anymore. Research commissioned by Facebook in 2011 revealed that of the company's then 721 million active users the distance between any two random people was 4.74 degrees. In 2008, it had been 5.28. Soon we will all have slept with each other. Your new girlfriend might have shagged half your Facebook friends or you might have shagged half of hers. Those who haven't been shagged are being slyly 'added' behind your back by these so-called 'friends'. I didn't have to train for months, buy expensive kit or pay summit fees to go on these adventures. The only equipment that mattered was my face, my body, my words, my heart and my capacity to take a risk.

And sucking you in, like the summit of Everest revealing itself after a storm, is the prize of love, an emotional glimpse of eternity. You may find love. Chances are you won't. But the important thing is not to die knowing that you wasted your time on this earth by not even attempting to get to it.

Yet my self-inflicted romantic entanglement with Keira and Phoebe and the ease with which I'd convinced myself that my life would be sorted out simply through finding the right woman made me realise that finding love was becoming an obsession – another to add to the pancake stack of them that had preoccupied me for years – and a convenient distraction from something I'd never really faced up to and which was my true unknown and that of virtually everyone I knew: being alone and *enjoying* being alone.

The last time I had truly felt alone, and exhilarated by it, had been in 2003 in the Yukon in far north Canada, on Lake Laberge outside Whitehorse with a team of huskies. There was nothing out there but the contrail of a distant jet in the refrigerated blue sky. Just wilderness. No sounds other than the crunch of snow under my feet and the panting of the dogs. For those few fleeting moments, contemplating the privilege of my total solitude, a place where it was easy to die with one misstep, the world just didn't matter. If it hadn't been for my family, I could have left it all behind.

So what did I really have to fear now? I was ready for it. I was writing in the morning, working out in the afternoon, going to my flat at night, eating basically and enjoying the simple routine. I was the healthiest I'd ever been. The OCD had flatlined as had the desperate need to do something, *anything*, with the dead time that had previously terrified me. I was knocking back dates and fuck-buddy invitations. I had resolved not to use women for sex. Most of all, I knew I was no longer one of *them*.

At Piazzolla and other cafés in Darlinghurst I'd meet examples of the misogynist Kristin had told me years before I was threatening to become. Single, separated or even married men with tablets or smartphones, guffawing at the latest smutty joke or batch of contraband celebrity orgy photos. Shop owners who'd habitually fuck their poorly paid immigrant female staff because they could get away with it. Ugly, bitter, scornful Rocco Siffredi fanboys who'd mingle on the street in the late afternoon sun assessing passing women like graded meat on a butcher's hook. These men would probably end up not just alone but chronically lonely, like the mad old coot who tied up his small dog outside the French patisserie on Victoria Street every evening and paced the footpath, nervously smoking, hoping to strike up a conversation with a stranger. Or the middle-aged woman, reputedly a virgin, who read the paper for hours outside Nectar's Hat every day on one coffee and sang carols in the same spot each Christmas. I think she did it more to remind herself that she belonged than for any spare change she got. Darlinghurst was full of these characters.

When the terrible news came through that Roger – a popular, strapping, physically fit, ebullient solicitor I'd see each day drinking coffee with his girlfriend at Piazzolla – had shot himself at home, aged just 44, I knew my priorities had to change. I wasn't going to leave this world without my daughter having seen the best of me. It was time to be a better father and focus on Evie, a girl who had been there with me through so many dramas and disruptions: the choke, Frankie's volatility, a conga line of dates, me running off overseas, the arrival of Keira, Lara's break-up with David and his instant replacement with another man who wasn't her father, losing our dog (it was hers too), being shunted off to the grandparents and my sister's, and not having a normal version of the one thing I wanted for her and I never had myself but could not provide: an intact family.

LAID BARE

She got through so much of it with heroic stoicism, quietly scribbling animals, holiday scenes, relatives and school friends in her sketchbook while her father's head was totally somewhere else.

One night, after fighting with Lara on the phone over something ultimately inconsequential, I'd lost my rag. It was a rare occasion for me to blow up after working so hard on my anger since the divorce, especially after the meltdown at Hawks Nest, but Lara, always a dogmatic person and possessing a volatile side of her own, still had a way of unsettling me like no one else.

I was in my room, fuming, when Evie walked in with a note. She smiled and handed it to me.

A COUPLE OF WAYS TO CALM YOUSELF

1. Breathe in and out 12 times.
2. Have a glass of water.
3. Think about the really long life ahead of you, dad.
4. Listen to light music.
5. Watch a funny TV show.
6. Remember that your part of a family.
7. Have some fresh air.
8. Go out for a long or short walk.

INTO THE UNKNOWN

9. Have a coffe, which is one of your favourite things, dad.
10. Meet up with a friend.
11. Have a two and a half sleep.
12. Turn the light off and meditate.
13. Read a book.
14. Rest.
15. Eat some fruit.
16. Go meet Ron.
17. Watch a movie on the computer in your bed.
18. Draw a picture.
19. Have pizza for dinner.
20. Buy a bottle of San Pellegrino. And again remember your part of a family.

Holding that piece of paper was like a revelation. I almost cried. Even the spelling mistakes and missing words were beautiful. Life really wasn't so hard. Happiness was there if I wanted it and simple to find. Evie had found her own ballast in what was left of the ruins of my marriage to her mother. I didn't need to listen to loud music or pump iron anymore to keep the OCD thoughts at bay or to fuck strangers to distract myself from the pain of being alone. The intermittent feelings of loneliness and frustration still sucked but, with a computer giving me access if not a true connection to the people I couldn't physically have in my life, I could cope with the solitude.

My little girl was far smarter than I was. She'd been through as much as I had, if not more. She'd lost a lot, too, but she was choosing to see the best in the situation. I wasn't. It was time to change. I owed it to her and myself.

In so many ways, because of the OCD, the dissolution of my relationship with Lara and my relentless quest to find a replacement, I'd been disconnected from my own child for her entire life.

Ernest Hemingway famously said: 'To be a successful father there's one absolute rule: when you have a kid, don't look at it for the first two years.'

I'd done that, literally, because of the OCD. But, somewhere along the line, two had become eight. I wasn't going to let it happen anymore.

After years of floating adrift, I'd landed.

* * *

Of all the challenges of coming out of divorce or a long-term relationship, probably the hardest one of all is resigning yourself to the possibility that there might not be another person out there for you at all, that your romantic life is not like a smartphone or a laptop or any other gadget you own:

it can't always be upgraded. What you had the first or second time around might be as good as it gets. And you have to not just resign yourself to that possibility but accept the fact that at some point in the future you are going to see or hear stories about your ex-wife or ex-girlfriend with other men. Men who could or should have been you. Time doesn't heal all wounds. You can't truly be friends with people you used to love. You've been programmed to think about them and react to them in a different way, even when you're no longer attracted to them. You just learn to disguise that feeling of loss better and be thankful for this new addition to your emotional armour.

You do what you can to stay attractive, hungry and good looking to strangers. You live for a sign of appreciation. You smile at girls on park benches or on the street, but time has caught up with you. You clip your pubes. Shape your eyebrows. The hair inside your nostrils and on your back and ears goes crazy but disappears from the top of your head. The grey begins its inexorable creep from the chin up. You're turning into your father. The women you desire aren't the ones who want you. But the older ones do. The ones who know you're imperfect and better for your knocks. The younger ones just think you're sad. You're likely better off without them but you always manage to convince yourself the 28-year-old with the Christy Turlington bod and the

Condoleezza Rice mind is waiting for you. Chances are she isn't. But you're not going to just settle for anyone.

Online facilitates fiction. Digital photography and image-correction trickery such as iPhoto, Hipstamatic and Instagram has sparked a narcissistic inferno that can never be put out. You only put up photos that make you look good, tag what you want people to see. All those new 'friends' don't see the mess you make of your car or your apartment. They're not there for the times you wake up in the morning, jam in your eyes, and wonder who the fuck is staring back at you in the bathroom mirror. But inside a computer you're a star. You embed the right music. You have glamorous girlfriends your mates would die to fuck. You say witty things. Your avatar has a much better life than you do.

The reality is that some nights you stay at home when everyone else is out and take photos of yourself on your laptop just to cut through the boredom. The things that entertained you in the past just don't pass muster anymore. Literature is dead. Television is moronic. Cinema just dresses up yesterday's shit. You can't be bothered with festivals. There's a reason why so many people can't go to them without taking drugs: the music's fucking terrible. You get to sleep batting off to European art porn or Lisa Ann gangbangs.

You go to the gym late on a Sunday night because you've got nothing else to do, then get home and work out again.

INTO THE UNKNOWN

The time you used to put into reading you now invest in sit-ups or bicep curls. You need to look good in that T-shirt. When you do manage to get out, you stand around drinking beer with the few mates you're still in touch with and you're not even sure what you're laughing at half the time or why the fuck you're friends with them in the first place, but you know it's important you're seen to laugh. You're a *bloke*.

We all want to be special. We all want to be cool. We all want to find love. But only some of us are cut out for finding it more than once, if at all. The rest of us have to make do with the fact we're unwanted, we're not half as good looking or interesting as we think we are and no one gives a fuck.

And, for me, this was my time.

* * *

I knew I'd lost my sexual mojo when in the spring of 2011 I went to a cousin's wedding in Woodend, a small town in rural Victoria, and my 63-year-old mother got laid and I didn't. We'd been sharing a room at a bed and breakfast and it had been a merry affair, lubricated with the powerful red wines of Bendigo and Heathcote. We were both plastered.

But when I woke the next day she was gone. I showered, dressed, and was drinking tea out on the deck when Sal, fresh from a double knee reconstruction and nursing a throbbing hangover, hobbled back into the room and collapsed on her bed. She was missing her pants. Half an hour later her one-night stand, a handsome, white-haired, recently widowed architect called Jerry, returned them on his way to the lobby. He'd discreetly rolled them under his arm. When she got back to Sydney he asked her out on a date. She accepted.

As with all weddings, the ceremony itself had been the least interesting part.

On the drive down Sal had opened up about her marriage to my father. I'd kept my distance from her for years for calling me a 'cunt' to Lara and trying to pair Lara off with Gully. Sal was no closer to an apology, but we'd still managed to repair our relationship without contrition on either side. We just agreed to disagree.

She told me she'd never really been in love with Alby – which she'd only fully understood with the benefit of hindsight and after years of personal growth in affairs with other men. She and Alby had been too young for such a commitment, were mismatched and knew nothing about the world. Once he'd got a ring on her finger, she felt he'd stopped trying to impress her. Immaturity and indolence: the faultlines of so many marriages, including my own.

Then at the reception I'd met Roslyn, the matriarch of a rich family who owned a chain of sex shops. The same age as my mother, she was attractive, frank about her adventures in bed and flirtatious. Yet she was in a sexless marriage with a man 20 years her senior, who wouldn't even get out of bed for birthday parties or weddings. He wasn't an invalid, just antisocial. Roslyn had a life totally separate from him. It seemed like such a waste. Why didn't she leave? Find another man she could laugh with, dance with and fuck behind the bushes? I suspected it was just the money, like so many other women I'd met.

'What for?' she replied. 'What would I do? Where would I have to go? I'm resigned to that part of my life being over.'

My arthritic mum, missing her pants and with the chance of a new beginning a few years shy of 70, was proof that wasn't the case. The difference between the two women was obvious. Sal was still taking risks. Roslyn wasn't.

* * *

Romantic love is rarely permanent. It can be. When transformed into the verb. But in its pure form typically it's short lived. A series of glimpses. When Lara turned to me all those years ago and said, 'I love you but I'm not in love with you' I should have said, 'What did you expect?' instead of breaking down and crying and tearing the house apart.

Love and relationships are two different things, if not diametrically opposed, but love (or lack of it) always gets used as an excuse to end a relationship. Some people are lucky and get durability *and* love. Some choose to stay in relationships without love. Some try to rekindle love that has already been lost. Some find a better kind of love even when they're in love.

A Perth friend of mine, Jason, was doing just that. He thought he had it all with his wife, his family, his beautiful contained little world, then met Therese, a woman he'd wanted all his life. She was married, had her own family and was similarly happy with her lot but the problem was she wanted Jason too. The glimpses were happening in the second reel of their lives, after 30 years of commitment to other people. But Jason and Therese didn't feel like they could start again and were too afraid to walk away from what they already had, too worried about what their kids would think, even though they were now adults. They *could* do it. But they weren't taking the risk.

'We decided to take the coward's way out and keep fucking each other and see what happens,' he told me, going into a second year of carrying on his dangerous liaison with Therese. 'No doubt we'll get caught and it will blow up anyway.'

So many marriages have failed because of both partners' expectation that love will endure and the glimpses will always be there. It's standard at any wedding for the words

INTO THE UNKNOWN

'celebration of our love' to be uttered. But under the trees in that garden in Woodend, seeing my cousin Nadine marry Keith, a nice young man she had known for ten years, I just felt cynical. I couldn't share their optimism. In my mind, marriage is not a celebration of love. It's a glorified tribute show to perseverance.

Marriage, again in my case, did its best to destroy love. When I look back on my decade with Lara, it was just a series of breakdowns in communication. The misread signals. The stupid jealousies. The fights. All with our differing expectations about roles and duties thrown into a thick, bubbling emotional gumbo cooking on top of an intense fire of anxiety and insecurity.

It only got worse when we divorced. We couldn't speak for two minutes on the phone before one of us had hung up on the other. Whatever messages we were trying to get across were still being lost even when there was nothing at stake.

* * *

Assertiveness in bed is the least of it. I did a national radio talkback show with the Australian writer Nikki Gemmell, the author of *The Bride Stripped Bare*, to talk about sex in long-term relationships. Gemmell seemed to think women generally weren't assertive sexually, which was news to me. That had never been a problem in my or any of my male friends' experience, especially with younger women. Straight in the tush? No problem. We're constantly shocked by what gets asked of us. Gemmell had been sexually liberated late in her adult life. She said she didn't care how her body looked. I had to bite my tongue. Partners commonly do, but they find it hard to bring up. It was a theme she continued in the book *Pleasure*. In the section 'What Men Want' she reprints a letter she received from an anonymous male.

> *Like you lot, we men are full of doubts, insecurities and fears about our attractiveness and desirability – but we'd rather die than admit it.*
>
> *We know you're afraid your bum looks too big but we really don't mind. So please, please don't turn the light off.*

Who is this phantom male? We'd rather die than say you have a fat arse.

Lara hadn't voiced her displeasure when I'd ballooned to Russell-Crowe-between-movies heft in the final few years of our marriage – Kmart polo shirts, turned-down baseball caps and all. I wished she had. Only long afterwards, through my mother, would I discover she'd stopped wanting to have sex with me. Lara's mother had blurted it out to Sal after we'd separated. If Lara had been more frank with me then it could well have saved our marriage. So much for 'in sickness and in health'. More a case of 'until you get fat and I get a better offer'.

Of course there are many complexities to long-term relationships. Men are loath to tell women that they are unhappy with their physical appearance. But what primarily drives male sexuality is just that: physical appearance. Men will do anything to avoid having to say what they really want to say. Which is that you can lose a few kilos. Your muffin top is becoming a problem. Your arms are wider than a paddle. You're not doing it for me anymore and the few times we fuck I'm actually finding myself thinking about someone else. There are men who will never leave their marriages because they have other reasons to stay: love that has been commuted to the realms of friendship and admiration, resignation that life 'gets in the way', or simple fear of being on their own. But they nurse their discontent like a testicular cyst. It's uncomfortable, a lot of the time they're in pain, yet they don't want to deal with it.

Why is it so taboo in a relationship to be open and honest about how we feel about a partner's physical appearance? Probably because the first reaction of so many women is to condemn those men who are so 'insensitive' as to face the issue directly rather than dance around it – or accuse them outright of sexism, objectifying women or, ridiculously, misogyny. Too often, criticising women honestly gets men stamped with the misogynist label when the plain truth is that a lot of women don't want to hear what men really think.

'Don't ever get into an argument with a woman, son,' Alby had been warning me since I was a teenager. 'You can never win.'

Women might say otherwise but in my experience straight talking on the subject of physical appearance is only acceptable to them when it's delivered on their terms or it validates the decision they've made in not going to the gym that day or having that third glass of wine.

'Let's go for a long hike together this weekend and for the next few weekends' is somehow considered acceptable but 'Babe, I'm concerned about your weight' is not, even though both can easily be misinterpreted. It's almost as if it's beneath our intellect to care about such things, even though physical attraction so often brings couples together in the first place and lack of it has an unerring habit of tearing them apart.

The carryover of so many marriages is becoming fat and unattractive. But vows, that certificate and one or two buns in the oven isn't insurance against being left. I made that mistake and paid the price. My weight obviously wasn't the primary factor in Lara's decision to leave, but it played a part (she'd later admit as much), just as my fight to get back to what I used to be got her intrigued again. If you don't make an effort with your health, diet and attitude to life during a long-term relationship or marriage, it is highly likely you will eat dust. That or you will need to make concessions to the fact that at some point your partner is going to be titillated by someone else. So keep them happy. Work out. Eat properly. Encourage flirting. Watch porn together. Go to a rub 'n' tug. Even consider having sex with other people, separately or as a couple or in a group. Reassess the value of monogamy, an often damaging and unrealistic imposition on a relationship when longevity is desired. Find new ways of relating to your partner. The key is doing whatever it takes to ensure that their emotional fidelity remains with you – and it applies to women and men alike. Women: don't complain about societal pressures of body image or the tyranny of the patriarchy. Men: no one gives a fuck about your biceps when they can see your gut. Just get off your arse, stop making excuses and make the necessary sacrifices.

Kids aren't a leave pass, either.

Rachel, a university lecturer in her mid-40s and mother of five with an eight-month-old baby and a husband with Asperger's (way more grief than she needed), had managed to retain the body of a woman half her age through good nutrition and regular yoga. The way the whole body-image debate – not unimportant when it came to combating the prevalence of eating disorders among young women and increasingly children – had become a new rallying point for feminists decrying the male 'subordination of women' stuck in her craw. She was livid about it.

'What's "empowering" about seeing cellulite on a woman's bum? Going for a run is more fucking empowering,' she complained over lunch at Piazzolla. She had a tuna salad. 'What bullshit. Personally I don't know how you can be fat being a mother of young children. How do they sit down all day? "Grow old gracefully"? What the fuck is that? What is graceful about fat? It's a disgrace. Their excuses and whingeing mean they are simply not vain enough. A bit of vanity is a good thing. Gore Vidal wasn't wrong. "A narcissist is someone better looking than you are." And spare me your "wisdom". It's hindsight with wrinkles.'

Another female friend also in her 40s, Polly, a Pilates instructor with a slender, toned body she'd worked hard at for 20 years and in a happy long-term relationship with a younger sculptor, said pretty much the same thing when I ran into her at the Wayside Chapel op-shop in Kings Cross. I'd been taking her classes and she was so much fitter than me. Her complaint was less with gawking men than with jealous women.

INTO THE UNKNOWN

'Oh, women are much worse than men,' she said while rummaging through the $1 book box. 'I walk down the street all the time and they stare at me like they're personally affronted. I'm like, "What's your problem, sister?" Get over it. *You* do something about your body.'

There are couples, of course, who aren't so shallow. An old friend of mine, Leon, had his face melt off in an accident when he was a young boy. He'd been playing with matches, his babysitter had left him and two of his friends in the car, and the vehicle had gone up in flames. His friends perished. He'd spent five years in hospital and more than three decades getting skin grafts. He had no hair, no nose, no ears, the tips of his fingers were missing, and he had a stoma in his throat so he could speak. He'd once been introduced to someone at a party who laughed and said, 'You can take off the mask.' But he'd married a beautiful young woman, Fiona, and they'd started a family together. They were on to their third baby the last time I ran into Leon. Fiona was inspirational to me. Her husband had always been inspirational. He was even staying in good shape when it would have been very easy of him to just let himself go and hide away. I don't think Lara had their courage. I hadn't had their courage. Very few people do.

Men aren't afraid of marriage or commitment. Nor are they driven by sex; that's a myth perpetuated by books such as *He's Just Not That Into You* and countless films, TV shows and magazine articles. The truth is they are just like women: driven by love. But they're happy to keep fucking until they find that glimpse of eternity.

The reason for that is simple. Men use sex as a diversion and form of self-validation because unlike women – who in my experience are emotionally and mentally stronger than men and have better support networks because they've always been encouraged to talk about their feelings – they don't cope terribly well with being alone. Women can live with their own company. Men by and large are terrified by it. Crudely put, they also don't stop screwing around until they get what they want, which is a woman they want to fuck forever or don't think they can top. Then they fall in love. If monogamy wasn't the unspoken but implicit clause of most long-term relationships, more men would emotionally commit to women they find less desirable and play around less. But monogamy, rightly or wrongly, is tied in inextricably with society's notions of love. So men are not about to fuck up the few shots they get at finding it.

It's why when you pick up gossip magazines and flick through the spreads of celebrity weddings, you never see a film star or athlete walk down the aisle with a girl with flabby arms or two chins, no matter how sparkling her personality might be. Generally if a man can get the babe, he will. The spectre of Jane Austen's Darcy has totally deluded generations of young women into thinking that even the most chivalrous men would rather seduce a woman over a period of months until the sexual tension becomes unbearable than fuck on the first or second date. They are rare creatures indeed. The vast majority of men are not initially drawn to a woman by character and personality over appearance. Wit, charm, intelligence, empathy, passion, kindness and goodness keep them interested, but physical attractiveness lures them in. Without it, the love we all want is fighting for survival.

* * *

Even with it, though, romantic love can also disappear. I hadn't expected it to happen when it did. It had taken so long. I thought it would never come. Lara dropped by my place one day to drop something off for Evie before school and when I looked at her the glimpse wasn't there anymore. It had just vanished. That portal to eternity had closed.

Nothing much about her had changed. She was still a vital, attractive woman – the Jessica Rabbit I'd fallen in love with all those years before. But I'd had a different kind of revelation. I no longer needed her affection or the ephemeral caress of a stranger to validate me. From thinking I wasn't good enough for Lara it dawned on me then that after everything I'd been through she might not be good enough for *me*. I still loved her, though, for who she was and what she meant to me and my daughter. She was a part of my life I couldn't erase and didn't want to erase.

I just stood there, wearing nothing but my underpants, scratching my three-day growth, not giving a damn about how I looked or thinking about what I should say – the sort of things I used to waste time worrying about.

I watched her lips move but I couldn't hear what she was saying. All I could hear was my heartbeat. My breath. I was thinking about who was on the decks at Piazzolla.

I'd mended my soul like I'd been told to do. Rebuilt my body, found peace. And learned to let go.

CHAPTER 14

A LITTLE PATIENCE

TRACK 14 'Welcome to the Club',
Joe Walsh, *So What* (1974)

Summer was coming after a dreadful winter. I was approaching my fifth year in Darlinghurst, half the length of my relationship with Lara. New bars and cafés were opening. St Vincent's Hospital was gobbling up more old terraces. The noise of power tools and construction workers, bothersome even on quiet days, was becoming more incessant. The pram-pushers and their white-collar husbands were moving in, having already drained the colour out of Newtown and Balmain. The junkies who should have perished over the cold months were still shuffling up and down Victoria Street like wounded Confederate soldiers at the Battle of Gettysburg, asking for spare coins, more indestructible than ever.

Change was all around. Giancarlo left Piazzolla to start his own place, Tutto Latte Express, in North Sydney, and found a girl closer to his age to move in with. His philandering days were over, a year shy of 50. 'I'm like Björn Borg. I quit at my peak,' he joked, with his usual modesty. Enrico had a second kid with his beautiful wife, Julie, and put Piazzolla on the market. Ron met a psychologist with three kids of her own and moved in with her and his two, bringing to an end the Divorced Fathers and Daughters All-Stars. Kristin accepted a huge redundancy payout from her bank job and started what it seems every creatively frustrated woman does at one point or another, an interior-decorating business. Isabella, whose Danish husband had put a gun under his jaw, found love again with a nice Jewish man, finished her cancer treatment and was getting ready for her one-year mammogram. Boyd the busker bought a new guitar, French made, with beautiful tone. He offered to come with me and buy one for Evie. My little girl, almost nine, didn't just have her mother's looks. She had her voice.

I was two years away from turning 40, an event of dread for some people but a beacon of hope for me. My 30s, outwardly a time of achievement and fulfilment, had for the most part been miserable, a litany of life challenges and horrors. But even though I was virtually bankrupt, my sportswriting career in Australia was over and I had nothing to show for myself while my friends were buying apartments or even second apartments, I was happier than I'd ever been. New opportunities were opening in my personal and professional life that would never have happened if I hadn't taken risks and put in the effort to wrest myself from the fate of just existing rather than living. The unfortunate business with SBS had proved a blessing: I was offered a new column with ESPN in South-East Asia, broke a story worldwide about the shady property dealings of a FIFA executive member, suddenly found my name appearing on Al Jazeera, the BBC and in the *Wall Street Journal*, and, best of all, discovered friends around the world I didn't know I had. As with Lara, calamity had morphed into opportunity. It had been a long road but one I'd had to take. I'd developed a prisoner's hardness in body and mind. I felt I could deal with anything. Even running into Frankie on the street.

'Hi, RDJ,' she said, tapping me on the shoulder from behind while I was walking through Kings Cross one day. She had a single bright orange slick through her blonde hair. 'You had coffee yet?'

On a new course of antidepressants and working a couple of days stretching canvases for a famous artist, her equanimity and openness made a nice change from being sprayed in the face with hazardous chemicals or screamed at in the street like a rapist. But we both knew we could never really be friends. She wouldn't leave her new boyfriend and come back, even though I suspected she still had feelings for me. The man stood to inherit millions. I had a collection of op-shop scarves and video-store fines. With him as a boyfriend or husband, she'd never have to stretch canvases for other people again. He'd just taken her to Cadaqués in Spain.

'Jacob and I are working on our relationship. I'm learning to do things differently,' she said. There was a long pause. 'The truth is he's asked me to marry him. I haven't said yes or no.'

I didn't know what to say. Even though I'd steeled myself for this moment and long ago resigned myself to having lost Frankie, I felt like the marrow was being sucked from my bones. What came out of my mouth was always going to be inadequate.

'You're getting *married*? But you never gave us a chance.'

'I said I don't know what's going to happen. There are some things that need to change.'

'Why would you marry someone you're not in love with? I know you're not in love with him. You'd be engaged by now. When someone asks you to marry them, you don't go away to think about it for a month. It's a yes or no.'

'I don't know about that. I'm not sure what I'm going to do.'

A LITTLE PATIENCE

'Why aren't you more romantic?'

'I'm not romantic. Don't have a romantic bone in me. Never have. The problem with you, Jesse, is you think life's a movie. It's not. At least, mine isn't.'

'There's no reason why it can't be, Frankie.'

She just rolled her eyes.

'I couldn't be a stepmum with you as a dad. I would have been the evil stepmother.'

'*Evil stepmother*? What *are* you talking about? I didn't choose to be a single dad. Evie comes with me. Just as Asperger's comes with you. I accept you for who you are. Why can't you just accept me for what I am?'

She looked away. She wasn't going there.

'Anyway, I want you to know I'm not pissed off with you anymore. You can have the painting back. It should be with you.'

After our Mexican stand-off and the ding-dong debate about moral ownership, she'd kept it just to spite me.

I got it back. She married in the spring.

* * *

While I was happy, my old friend Gully – the handsome, towering, athletic firefighter Sal had once tried to set up with Lara – was in a bad way. His wife, the mother of his two boys, aged eight and seven, had walked out on him 18 months before after 15 years together , saying he didn't 'give' enough in the relationship and in the bedroom and that she wasn't 'stimulated'. Gully was still very much in love with her, as I had been with my wife in those first few years after the break-up, and wracked with guilt in thinking it had all been his fault.

Gully's way of dealing with his pain, as with so many men faced with the same terrible situation, was to distract himself. He'd jump out of planes. Dive off cliffs. Get tattoos. Run marathons. Go canyoning. Search for Aboriginal art in the bush. Fuck strangers on adult personals sites. Mow his neighbours' lawns, even aerate them with a pitchfork. He wanted to enter the Sydney to Hobart yacht race with me – which was ridiculous enough – but then upped the nutty quotient by suggesting we pilot a tinny to New Zealand. The last time I'd been in a boat, a Thai junk for the funeral at sea of the legendary circumnavigator and ladies' man Sir David Lewis, whose memoirs I'd worked on, I'd thrown up even before we'd got out of Sydney Heads.

And when he couldn't leap off or out of things anymore or afford another tattoo or fuck another bored single mother with his dick swaddled in rubbers, Gully raided the liquor cabinet, finishing off whole bottles of whisky or vodka in a sitting, and going to work the next day to save lives while he could barely function in his own. Anything to dull the pain of the awareness that after all this time, after all the emotional investment he'd made in that relationship, in fatherhood and right on the cusp of his 40s, he was just like me: alone. Another child of the 1970s who'd wanted to prove his divorced parents wrong but been proven wrong himself. Marriage, at least the idea of it, was dead for both of us.

Gully pined for his family. He told me he still wanted to grab his wife every time he saw her, shake her and tell her to wake up from the bad dream they were both in. But he resisted the temptation. His hope was that if he deliberately ignored her and showed no interest at all in what she was doing she'd come to him eventually and admit she'd been wrong.

It didn't work, of course. She'd promptly found herself a new man. A copper. What is it with police and other men's wives?

'I now understand what you went through,' he told me one afternoon, late on a Saturday, casting a line off the jetty at my mother's holiday house at Wisemans Ferry, north of Sydney. We sometimes went up there just to get away from the men we were in the city. To drink. Run through the bush, sometimes for hours. Work out with tyres and ropes. Burn stuff. Gully was almost closer to Sal than I was. He could fix things; I couldn't.

'I feel like killing that bastard, I really do,' he said, swigging his beer. 'I'm sorry I wasn't there for you, man.'

'Not a lot of people were. They never are. Everyone's dealing with their own shit. Fuck, I'm not a saint. You don't know how it feels until it happens to you.'

'It's just the constant pain I can't handle. It's still there even when I've done everything I can think of doing. I joined a fucking surf club. I'm going to Bikram yoga. I'm trying to meditate. The other day I got invited to a gangbang. I'm thinking of going. What else is there to do? It's more than mental. It's physical. Like I've got bile or acid welling up in my stomach. I can't sleep. I'm on edge. I find myself laughing at the ridiculousness of how I'm feeling – it's such a fucking cliché – when I'm not crying. I can't see a way through it. I just want her back.'

'No, you don't. Trust me. You gotta let go.'

'I don't know how.'

'Go to that gangbang. Run. I dunno, Gull. Do whatever you can. Time takes care of the rest.'

'The problem is I don't know what I'm doing half the time.'

'I don't know what I'm doing half the time, either. You think any bloke in our situation knows what the fuck they're supposed to be doing?'

'I guess.'

A LITTLE PATIENCE

'You're not really doing anything I haven't done. Hopefully you just won't make my mistakes.'

'She's a good woman, even though sometimes I don't even think she's a nice person. I still love her. I don't want to let go. I can't let go.'

'You will. Listen to my mother. She loves you like a son. She wanted to give you my wife. Now let's fish.'

But, like the women in our lives, nothing was biting.

* * *

Back in Sydney, my dating life was dying a slow death.

I went out to a wine bar in Surry Hills with Athena, an attractive real estate agent in her late 20s who revealed to me after our second bottle that she had a prosthetic foot. She'd lost the original in a lawnmower accident playing in her backyard when she was three and by her own admission had spent most of her adult life searching for a father figure in her relationships, which was about the only way I could account for her agreeing to take me to bed. I tried not to look down throughout.

Her dad had blamed himself for the accident and the only way he could deal with the guilt was to be distant with her. If he got too close, the torment of having accidentally butchered his own child would flood him. It was a sad tale but familiar. I had detached from Evie because of the OCD. But I had got on top of it and reconnected. Her father hadn't.

Athena, however, wouldn't reconnect with me when I suggested we be friends after our one-night stand. Because of the frequent lulls in conversation – not the missing foot – we weren't cut out to be lovers. But I liked her enough to think we might offer each other something beyond sex. She delivered it to me straight.

'I don't think you're someone I'd like to be friends with.'

'Why?'

'You didn't pay for the wine.'

'But you put down your card and said, "I'm getting this one." I expected we'd have a second date. I was going to pay next time. What's the problem?'

'Well, it says a lot about the kind of man you are that you agreed. Obviously your regard for women is low. No man has ever let me pick up a bill on a first or any date.'

'So if you were so offended why'd you come home with me?'

Athena didn't have an answer for that. Is it any wonder so many men are confused about what goes on inside the heads of women?

* * *

A LITTLE PATIENCE

I tried again with a 25-year-old, six-foot-tall model called Beatrice I'd met through Facebook. The first date went well. When she proposed we get together again and I come by her apartment in North Bondi the following Sunday I thought I was destined to be a cult hero to men under 177cm everywhere. But when she opened the door she was clutching some fire-twirling sticks.

'You're serious?'

'Yes, you *must*. You'll have the hang of it in a couple of weeks. A lot of people do it around Bondi.'

Well, of course they did. Bondi was bursting at the seams with long-haired fuckwits in beanies.

Beatrice wanted us to take our twirling sticks to the end of her street. Out onto a windswept headland in the middle of a tempest. I half-heartedly twirled one of the sticks and dropped it to the ground, defeated not just by the task but my existence. What was I doing? Why was I here? Had it come to this? We could have been drinking, talking, fucking, *anything*. Instead I was out on the street, getting saturated, fumbling with a piece of wood. Chasing the girls of my past wasn't getting me anywhere. The idea of having sex with them appealed. But then what? Was it really worth going there? Beatrice was attracted to my profile photo, the other me, her ridiculous Hank Moody fantasy, but didn't know the first thing about the real man in front of her or, it seemed, even want to find out. She wanted to play Surfer Girl and twirl a fucking stick.

* * *

I didn't have such a problem with Justine. She understood me straightaway. We met sitting at adjoining tables in a café in Kings Cross. I complimented her on the Yves Klein-blue pants she was wearing and we began talking. She wouldn't tell me her age but I guessed she was in her early 50s. A gallery owner, she was the sexiest woman I'd met for a long time. Witty, intelligent, in shape, full lips, venturesome eyes. I was smitten. We paid for our coffees separately and virtually the next moment we were back at my flat, her car in a one-hour parking spot, fucking.

Justine gave more passion and me more pleasure in that hour we were together than I'd had in a dozen hook-ups with women half her age. I checked my watch. The meter was almost up. She put on her clothes, kissed me at the door and got back to her car with two minutes to spare.

Only afterwards would I realise that it was one of the few times since I'd rubbed against Lara's back all those years ago that I hadn't found someone to fuck through a dating site or from being added as a friend on Facebook. Justine was a complete stranger. And I'd seduced her – and her, me

A LITTLE PATIENCE

– after an innocuous comment in a café. Just plain attraction and chemistry. There wasn't a future for us as a couple, we both knew that, but we'd take this encounter for what it was and treasure it for its simple beauty.

I was on my way back to real life. Of sorts.

* * *

I was also clawing back some of my lost dignity.

When an old school friend, Hannah, a mother of two in a failing marriage, asked me unexpectedly – after some catch-up drinks at the Darlo Bar – to 'take me home and fuck my brains out', I walked away. I wanted her to save her marriage and find more glimpses with her husband, if that was at all possible. I wanted her kids to have what my child couldn't: a family that stayed together. It was up to her to leave him. Not for me to give her an excuse to separate.

'I'm not ever going to be the "other guy", Hannah,' I said, feeling as hard and resolute as Clint Eastwood.

I hadn't got to be the avenging hero when I'd confronted David. But I'd finally found my own kind of moral revenge.

* * *

Online, the same players were out in force with new sets of photos and tighter T-shirts, trying to pass themselves off as good men but fooling no one except the fresh batch of innocents who'd had their hearts broken over the winter and were looking for someone just to spoon them and tell them everything was going to be alright. Out of boredom and curiosity I occasionally logged on to my old profile and kept it active, but more than anything I was fascinated by the lies these men traded in. I was seeing it all differently now, from the other side.

Online dating had helped me through the worst period of my life and made me feel desired and valued again when I really had lost the will to go on and could see no future for myself without my family. I'd also been lucky enough to make some genuine, lasting friends out of women I'd cast aside for various superficial reasons when I was a red-eyed dating vampire getting off on all the female attention and out of control with my own vanity. Those women were and remain far better people than I will ever be. But ultimately, as I was belatedly to realise, the pleasures of online dating were fleeting and unfulfilling. More than anything it had given me licence to betray the good man I'd once been. I'd opportunistically fibbed and misrepresented my intentions to women as much as anyone. Reading the profiles, I was struck by the self-recognition. It takes a thief to catch a thief.

A LITTLE PATIENCE

'I'm a fun-loving guy who tries not to take life too seriously.'

'I'm really new to internet dating.'

'I'm trustworthy, honest, kind and down to earth.'

'I was brought up to respect others and see the good in all people.'

'I'm finding it difficult to find the right girl for me.'

'I'm a glass-half-full kind of guy.'

'I'm seeking new experiences and new friends.'

Endless blather. Endless bullshit. Put on a blindfold. Pick up a dart. Throw. You'll hit a player.

But one profile stood out to me above all the others. David's. It was most illuminating. My ponytailed assailant was freshly single after a 'long-term relationship' and had been raised 'with good morals and an old-fashioned sense of ethics'. In the bit about physical activities he'd even put: 'Walking my dog.'

I briefly considered sending him a kiss.

* * *

It was a Wednesday afternoon. I was taking Evie and her cousin Haley, a bright ten-year-old with a Sinéad O'Connor haircut, to swimming lessons. We were at an intersection in Leichhardt, with traffic banked up in all directions. I wanted to be out of the car, back in Darlinghurst, away from the suburban garboil I had left all those years before. Far from hating the east, leaving it now ratcheted up my anxiety. I was clenching the wheel tightly.

'Leichhardt sucks,' I said, grimacing.

'There's traffic in Darlinghurst, you know,' said Haley.

'Not like this.'

Then Evie spoke up.

'You know, Dad, you could try a little patience. Then you might find life gets easier.'

Half a decade on from the rupture, my little girl, like that ambulance driver outside Lara's house, was giving me some hard-earned advice. I liked to think I had seen it all as a kind of 'war journalist', as one girlfriend put it, but Evie, an unwitting passenger on that journey, had seen it all, too. She'd probably learned more.

My gorgeous, smart, wise young daughter was already showing that she'd grow up a more stable adult than me. I hoped she would think I'd been a good father.

And even if I wasn't, I'd tried to be.

* * *

Is it possible to love too much? The answer's yes. I discovered that the hard way. Some time after Lara left me, on one of the few occasions she tried to express her feelings in words, she'd put it this way: 'I know you love me and loved me desperately but that was exactly the problem.'

I'd been a weight on my wife, just as I had been with Frankie. When my heart latched on to another human being I managed to kill off the very love that gave it life. I was my own worst enemy. And I wasn't alone. Whether it was Ron or Gully or any of the other men I knew who were recovering from having their wives or girlfriends leave them, we were going through the hardest time of our lives because we had loved without the brake on, not thinking we'd ever crash. Our marriages weren't supposed to fall apart. *Ever.* But they had, far too easily. Had we taken it all for granted? Was that the problem?

There is something to be said for men and women in long-term relationships or marriages living separately. Like the Australian broadcaster Derryn Hinch and his wife, Chanel, his fourth. They reside in separate apartments in the same block in Melbourne. Or film director Tim Burton and actress Helena Bonham Carter, who live in adjoining townhouses in London. But most of us don't have the financial wherewithal to do that. We live, especially in cities, in tiny spaces, paying way beyond our means for the privilege. When you add kids, pets, TVs, computers, tablets, phones, in-laws and toilet-seat politics on top of the normal stresses of everyday life, it's a wonder any relationships survive at all. That's because the natural consequence of most relationships is cohabitation: frequently napalm to romance.

Men who love too much 'suffocate' their partners. Men who love too little are not 'giving' enough. We all go looking for the middle ground but too often end up somewhere totally off track, wracked with confusion and self-reproach. By the time we twig how to get it right, we've lost the one we love. That's what happened to me.

It had well and truly sunk in that I overcompensated with the women I loved because of my fear of losing them. But I also knew I wasn't afraid of falling in love all over again, even if that would subject me to the same challenges I'd faced getting those glimpses of eternity with Lara and Frankie. There was still time for me and I didn't want to make the same mistake again. Living and not existing demanded nothing less.

My friend Kirk, who'd wanted to kidnap Bosco from David and came by Piazzolla late most afternoons from his publishing job in the city to take his place among the Darlinghurst Council of Elders, had never fallen in love and didn't expect to. He just wanted to fuck girls. 'Lay some pipe.' Line 'em up like a cab rank. And he was 40, outwardly normal, in an office surrounded by women and with plenty to offer the right girl but, unlike me, deadened inside. He'd been doing it for 20 years. He'd never married, never known the joy of trying for a baby in a state of love, much less the wonder of even being in love. Kirk would just shrug his shoulders and argue that relationships were an outdated, abhorrent concept.

'If Christopher Hitchens had lived longer, he'd have written a polemic on the myth of relationships,' he told me.

Of course, Hitchens, the late and great contrarian, had been married twice and fathered three children. He must have seen some value in them.

Kirk even conceded that he might rethink his position if Heidi Klum miraculously walked into Piazzolla. In the end, like so many men, it all came down to finding a woman he wanted to fuck for the rest of his life or getting to a point where he didn't think he could do any better.

I'd only played for a short time, for just a few years, and I'd ended up hating it. I'd come to love another woman, Frankie, but I missed having a wife. Spooning Lara in the mornings before going to work. Talking about what holidays we'd take. Cooking for her. (I hadn't cooked for so long; it's easier and sometimes cheaper when you're single to eat out every night, and it's better to be around people – even if you're on your own.) Having her beauty products in the bathroom, neatly arranged, some still in their original boxes, and not just my razor. The smell of sandalwood in our bedroom. The flowers she bought. The way she'd arrange pillows on the sofa or tea candles on the mantel over the fireplace. The way she made me feel part of something more important than myself until depression and OCD engulfed me. She was, to all intents and purposes, *home*.

On the rare occasions I was invited inside Lara's flat, now denuded of all traces of David, I'd see things that had once been ours: old pictures, rugs, throws, pieces of furniture. Their familiarity winded me. But they were arranged differently. They were solely hers now. It left me with a bizarre sensation that I found difficult to process: I felt connected to the space and the things in it but disengaged from her, even though at Christmas time, unsettlingly, she still spoke of me and Evie as her 'family'.

We even went out to dinner, again, to a cheap Thai restaurant in Kings Cross, and this time managed not to fight. My anger had long since subsided and she didn't have to threaten to involve the long arm of the law. We conversed like old friends, Evie happy to see us put aside our enmities. I talked about Frankie and Keira. She told me all about David and Wes. Another full circle.

I couldn't help myself and remarked, unfairly, because I didn't know him, that Wes didn't seem to be the kind of man who was going to stimulate her for the rest of her life.

'There were times, Jesse, when you'd come home from work, go upstairs to bed and I honestly thought I'd walk in to find you'd topped yourself,' she said. Lara looked like she was about to cry. 'I felt all alone. All I've ever wanted is someone nice to take care of me.'

It was true. I hadn't been able to do that when it mattered. I thought I was able to do it now, but it was too late. I'd let her down and she me. We couldn't go back. Too much cruelty from both sides. We could never be whole again. We were here like this, splitting a $55 bill, because we both loved our daughter and had found a space where we could almost be friends. And Evie, stuck between us, two halves of a failed marriage, would grow up, just like we both had, thinking she could do it better.

As her father, I hoped with all my heart she would. Just like Alby had hoped for me. Sooner or later one of us was going to figure it out.

* * *

Looking back, it was inevitable. Old habits die hard. But this time I hadn't gone looking for her. She'd come looking for me.

Her name was Tori and she sent me an email on the same site I'd met Sunny to tell me she'd been drawn to me, for some unfathomable reason, in a 'sea of men'. There *was* a sea. The Pacific Ocean. All 12,000 kilometres of it between Sydney and where she lived, Los Angeles, a city in which I'd spent all of three days after the misadventure in San Francisco. Just about the most benighted place for relationships in the whole world. Jokes about the poverty of love in LA are an industry in itself.

I'd liked it, though. The sushi was big. The vintage stores were great. The mannequins had incredible racks. And at least in LA they actually tried to make good coffee while the rest of America still didn't have a clue and didn't care. Just as the eastern suburbs of Sydney had repelled me at first, only to get under my skin, something about the unashamed venality of LA perversely appealed. I took Tori and the city itself as a challenge.

Her appeal was more straightforward. She was as glamorous as a Kennedy wife: a classic blonde, 32 years old, tall, with a gymnast's body, fine features, a graceful neck and perfect teeth. Like me, she had gone through a shitty divorce to a muso and had lost her dog in the break-up. She told me she was vulnerable. She'd recently been dumped by an Australian record producer and was 'processing' her pain.

It was Tori's eyes above all else that won me over, though. I knew it from just one look. They were dark, knowing, wondrous, framed by eyebrows as beautiful as the brushstroke of a Sufi calligrapher. I'd seen thousands of faces on the internet but I knew she was worth leaving Australia for once again. She didn't have an exotic sideline, like burlesque

A LITTLE PATIENCE

dancing or escorting. She produced TV commercials. She was a regular, straight-up girl from Wisconsin – except for the exceptional and somewhat unsettling detail that she'd gone out with one of the biggest movie stars in the world, Bradley Cooper from *The Hangover* movies. It threw me totally when she told me. Finding love on the internet or anywhere else for that matter is hard enough without the added pressure of your prospective girlfriend having shared long walks with 'THE SEXIEST MAN ALIVE!'.

I had to play this one differently, not least because after I'd told her of my previous trips overseas to meet women Tori became suspicious of my motives. She was cautious. She talked of not 'disappearing down the rabbit hole' too quickly.

'Babe, I'm thrilled you're coming but I'm starting to wonder if this is a pattern for you,' she said after I'd booked my ticket to LA. 'You know, feeling so "certain" about someone. But then it fades and moves on to someone else. Getting wrapped up in the excitement of it all, the drama, the romance. I'm worried that this is more about the adventure of it than how you feel about me.'

I didn't think it was, though it may have appeared that way. The only pattern I could see was my resistance to settling for anything less than a glimpse. It was impractical, it was costing me money I didn't have, it wasn't the most ideal situation for me or Tori and especially my daughter but, unlike with all the other women I'd been with since Lara and Frankie, it felt right. We even got around to talking about how Evie might break up her year, going to school in Sydney and coming to LA for holidays. That was the only thing that didn't sit right for me. Seeing even less of Evie would be hard. But I was so focused on finding love, glimpsing eternity, that I was even prepared to sacrifice time with my child. When I told Lara about my plans, she reacted in a way I hadn't anticipated: she said she felt she was having a 'midlife crisis'.

'You had one of those years ago,' I joked.

I didn't want a relationship that was about convenience or constructed on admiration. That was too easy. It wasn't about sex, either. That had long ago ceased to be a motivation in my life. I wanted a connection. I wanted love. And I was never going to apologise for that or compromise trying to find it, like so many people do, as if it's some sort of grand indulgence to be found on the upper shelves of Abraham Maslow's hierarchy of needs. Love is never an indulgence. It's as essential to the true meaning of life as breathing and eating.

The trips to see Olivia in New York and Sunny in San Francisco and Keira's flight from Greece had taught me something. I wasn't going to profess love to someone I hadn't met in person, even though when Tori and I chatted late into

A LITTLE PATIENCE

the night on Skype and we spent vast stretches of time just looking at each other I felt overwhelmed by a desire to tell her I loved her. I even typed the words 'I love you' as an IM but couldn't bring myself to touch the 'Return' key.

I was going to do as Evie said: try a little patience. I was going to wait for the glimpse, not pre-empt it because I'd become addicted to a feeling. That's what I told myself, anyway.

This time, I wanted it to be real.

CHAPTER 15

LET THE RIGHT ONE IN

TRACK 15 'Paradise City', Guns N' Roses, *Appetite for Destruction* (1987)

In 2004 Joseph Kaye, a computer science student at Cornell University, came up with a software development project called 'Virtual Intimate Objects' in which a red dot was installed on the desktops of ten couples in long-distance relationships. Designed to be deliberately low-bandwidth and kept as simple as possible, VIO's sole purpose was to communicate intimacy. One person would click on the dot and it would redden on the computer of their partner, fading to transparent over a period of hours only if they didn't click it again. Some of the participants in the VIO project would click the dot 800 times a day, but the average was 35. Just seeing the dot turn red made them feel connected.

By 2012, those couples didn't need red dots. They had Facebook pokes. When I asked Tori before I got to LA why she felt the need to poke me countless times a day without sending me a personal message in a text or an email, she said it was her way of 'letting you know I'm thinking about you'.

In the age of social media, who needs the beauty of language when we can jab each other with virtual sticks? We're going back to being a planet of apes.

* * *

I was more nervous than usual.

There was the Bradley Cooper factor, of course, and the fact that Tori had been playing it cooler with me than I'd liked, but the real reason wasn't hard to figure out: the way I was feeling about it, this girl was my last throw of the dice. My love life was turning into romantic tourism. I didn't want to go back to dating in Sydney. Evie was growing older. She needed me to have my shit sorted, to have the next stage of my life mapped out. For me that meant with a woman beside me. Even if, being with Tori, it meant us being apart for several months a year.

The guys at Piazzolla were across every small detail of my campaign to turn up in America looking my best. The afternoon before I left for LA I took a seat with the

Darlinghurst Council of Elders, who were already deep in conversation. The subject, as always, was sex.

'If you're going to fuck an inanimate object, I always say reach for an avocado,' said Quentin, a conceptual artist.

'Doesn't it, like, fall apart in your hands?' said Kirk, one table away. 'Surely a mango's the go?'

'Not in my experience. Never had a problem. Another good lay is clay.'

'Clay?'

I chimed in. 'I had it off with a leather couch once. Was 14 or 15. My teenage years were hard times. I fucking loved that couch.'

'Rather you loved fucking it. You still got it?' said Quentin.

'I wish I did. Kept it as long as I could but Lara threw it out.'

'What? She knew?'

'I'm sure she suspected something.'

I was asked to lift up my shirt and show the Elders the abs and 'Beckham lines' I'd been working so hard to achieve by running close to a half marathon each day, working out at my makeshift bush training camp at Wisemans Ferry and eating nothing but kangaroo meat and eggs. It still amazed me that I hadn't even been able to see my dick because of my belly just five years before.

'You wax your chest, Fink?' said Enrico.

'Wax? Fuck no. Clipped it. Beard trimmers. And my ears. Back. I'm a fucking hair plant. I even shaved my arse for the first time.'

'I'm an arse shaver going way back,' interjected Paulie, a carpenter.

Kirk looked intrigued. 'You shaved your arse, Fink? Razor or clippers?'

'Clippers.'

'Me too,' said Paulie, laughing. 'And I'm Lebanese. Nothing wrong with a bit of backburning. Amazing how much just *falls* to the floor.'

Louie, a bartender and soon-to-be first-time father, took me aside after I'd paid for my farewell coffee. He threw an arm around my shoulders.

'Brother, just by getting on that plane you're chasing your dreams. It's *living*. What more of us would like to do or just never get the chance or let slip by. Enjoy yourself, you mad bastard.'

* * *

I drove over to Lara's to say goodbye to Evie. When I pulled up in the car she was playing with kids across the road at a neighbour's house, kids I hadn't seen before. She was taller than all of them, saturated in water from a garden hose.

There was a backyard party going on. Lara came out of the house, glass of wine in hand.

'Come have a drink before you go,' she said. 'Just one.'

We sat down between a woman we didn't know, with other strangers, filling them in on our care arrangements and making small talk about work, school and summer's usual spate of shark attacks. Apropos of nothing the woman suddenly made an observation, aided by a third or fourth sauvignon blanc.

'I'm sorry. But I have to say it. It's obvious to me you still love each other.'

Lara just looked at me, silently, for half a minute before she took the conversation somewhere else. We smiled at each other. It was a wistful exchange. The most profound moment we'd shared since the separation. We did love each other. We always would, but it was too late now. I hadn't been able to convince her over the intervening years that I was the man she fell in love with.

Gully phoned me at the airport. He'd just had another joyless, anonymous internet hook-up.

I told him what had happened with Lara.

'Interesting. Could you ever go back?'

It had been five years since our break-up. We'd divorced.

'I don't know, mate. I want this to work with Tori, I really do, but I also want Evie in my life. I want to be with her every day. But the only way for that to happen is to go back to Lara. I just can't see it working. I feel paralysed around her. I love her and I resent her. I don't know what to do.'

On the plane over I watched a movie called *Crazy Stupid Love*, which resonated with me like few others I'd recently seen. Steve Carell's character, Cal, is left by Emily (Julianne Moore), his wife and the mother of his children, after she has an affair. He wisens up to how he might win her back through the help of a debonair womaniser (Ryan Gosling) he meets in a bar, makes himself attractive again, sleeps with multiple other women and finds inner peace – but won't give up on the dream of winning her back. Though reconciliation is presented as a possibility, there is no neatly tied-up ending. There never is.

* * *

In the arrivals hall holding a white cardboard sign stood quite possibly the most physically intimidating woman I'd ever laid eyes on.

SWF SEEKING SWM
LOOKING FOR A PERSPICACIOUS, WITTY,
KIND, SEXY, INTELLIGENT, ATHLETIC, WARM,
CREATIVE MAN WITH A GREAT SENSE OF HUMOR.
A MAN WHO KNOWS WHAT HE WANTS AND

LAID BARE

> ISN'T AFRAID TO GO AFTER IT. A PENCHANT FOR SCARVES AND FINE WINE IS A MUST AND SPONTANEITY AND A SENSE OF ADVENTURE IS A BONUS. IF YOU ALSO HAPPEN TO BE AN INCREDIBLE FATHER?
> WELL, SOLD.

It was one of the most endearing things a woman had ever done for me. Life *was* a movie. I was blown away. There was one problem, though: Tori wasn't just alien-beautiful with her short blonde hair, cat eyes and Frank Gehry-designed cheekbones – she was alien *tall*. When I went to kiss and hug her, the cap on my head got knocked off on her décolletage. So stratospheric, in fact, was she in her killer heels that she made me feel like I was Dudley Moore to her Susan Anton. Driving to West Hollywood in Tori's immaculate car back to her immaculate apartment I found myself unwittingly cracking jokes in an Arthur Bach accent. She was on another level to anything I'd ever experienced in all my years of dating women. Her perfection and order terrified me. When I walked through her front door and set down my bags I noticed she'd sectioned off her bookshelves into subject areas.

I showered, we had sex (the best I'd had in years), and the first day was everything I'd hoped for. That was the easy part. Connecting with her, though, in the days that followed was a different proposition. After we'd make love, Tori couldn't keep her hands off her iPhone. Every minute she was texting someone, answering questions I wasn't privy to. *Are you alive? How was it? How was he? Is he everything you hoped for? Is he The One?* I could only guess. She didn't let me into that part of her private life.

I'd spoon her and she'd stay rigid. I spent more time looking at her shoulderblades than into her eyes. Everything that was happening between us felt like it was coming from my end. The sex was electric but always initiated by a first touch from me. Tori looked at me affectionately, she laughed at the right moments, even got my Australian sense of humour, but the incidental kisses and caresses one expects from a lover in a place of true intimacy weren't forthcoming. I'd get the occasional gentle hug or peck, but nothing more. The only theory I could come up with was that I just wasn't doing it for her. I felt like an intruder in her apartment. She was so distant from me emotionally, I didn't know what to say to her, how to find a way into her soul. After being in the States only a short time our four-month internet love affair felt like it had counted for nothing. I couldn't understand why she wasn't opening up to me. I was an anxious wreck.

Why was she was pulling back? She said I was attractive, that we had chemistry. We had the same values, the same hopes for the future. So what did she want? What was I lacking? Was I too short? Was it my snaggly teeth? Was the ghost of Bradley Cooper fucking up what I saw (at least at the time) as my one last shot at happiness?

And then it hit me: perhaps Tori was sizing me up as the father of her child. She was so beautiful and had so many options available to her that she could afford to be cold as ice. The same thing I'd done to so many women myself.

'You have to understand, Jesse, I'm only just getting to know you,' she told me when I asked her why she wouldn't touch me the way I was touching her.

I didn't listen. 'I'm a tactile person, Tori. I don't understand. I've spent every hour of every day for months thinking about you and waiting to come here. I thought we had something already.'

'What? Sex isn't intimate enough for you? It's intimate for me.'

'No. That's not intimacy.'

'I've known you for four months but you have to realise I only met you four days ago. There's a *process*. Four days is not enough time to fall in love with someone. I'm enjoying getting to know you and discovering the real person you are. You only get to know that side when I see you in my space, which is why I'm enjoying having you in my space. I want to see you not at your best. I'm enjoying having you here and doing stuff with you.'

Everything but touching me.

I couldn't believe I'd fooled myself all over again into thinking this time it would be any different. But what a fool believes, he sees.

* * *

We spent the rest of the week exploring LA in Tori's car and trying to find some cadence in whatever it was we had. She took me to Malibu, the boardwalk at Venice, Topanga Canyon, a Trader Joe's supermarket stocked with blueberry punnets the size of baseball mitts, a Korean restaurant where all the waiters were Mexican, a hipster café where the friendly barista tipped me off that if I wanted an Australian-style strong flat white it was advisable to order a 'double cappuccino without the foam'. Valuable advice that could have saved me a whole lot of trouble on my two previous trips to America.

Sooner or later the world is going to be overrun by hipsters writing screenplays on MacBooks. In fashionable LA cafés, ostensibly Apple stores styled like speakeasies, everyone is working on a script – or fucking around on their Facebook pages or Twitter accounts while they should be working on a script. Even the newspapers are filled with ads promising successful writing careers featuring hipsters working on MacBooks. Tori pointed out that even with the beaten-up black-leather cover on my laptop, a machine she'd christened 'The Ragged Mac', I was one of them too. The truth in the statement pained me.

We're all trying to be different and so desperate to be noticed that somehow we've arrived at a point in human evolution where buying a $150 T-shirt covered in holes and someone else's stains is considered a sign of individualism rather than rank stupidity. Those who go out of their way to set themselves apart – surfer boys with their bleached hair and Pashtun beards, rocker girls with their Betty Page haircuts and full-sleeve tattoos – are just drawing more attention to the fact that there's nothing original or interesting about them at all. The truly interesting people are the ones who don't stand out. Anonymity is far more intriguing.

LA, as I fully expected it would be, wasn't that different to the eastern suburbs back home. The shirtless guys walking backwards uphill in Runyon Canyon wouldn't have been out of place on the Bondi to Bronte walk. The only waivers for beauty in this city were fame and money. When on one hike Tori and I passed a panting, fossilised old codger who looked like Jerry Garcia, she grabbed my arm.

'That was my best friend's ex-boyfriend.'

'Who? Hannah? Really? *Him*?'

Hannah was a beautiful young Jewish woman. She would have been half his age.

'Yeah, he's worth a lot of money. Buys a lot of art. Drops $60,000 a time.'

There seemed to be two kinds of people in LA: those who were dying to make it and those who had already made it but were afraid of losing their relevance. It struck me as a brutal place for any relationship to begin or survive.

About as brutal as it was for comedians.

At the Laugh Factory on Sunset Boulevard, one of Tori's friends, Simon, a film and TV actor who'd most recently had a small role in the fifth season of *Californication*, did a sweet routine of new material about his baby son. It died. When another comedian got up and did jokes about ugly kids getting knocked back by rapists and being molested with wire hangers he got the biggest laughs of the night. Simon came up to me afterwards and apologised. I just wanted to hug him.

Being flawed is good for comedy, intolerable in relationships.

* * *

Despite trying to stay positive, I could feel my dream of finding love slipping away. No matter what I did, Tori wouldn't let down her guard. She'd chide me when I complained about how much time she spent on her iPhone (something I didn't own, and didn't want to) and compared my stubbornness to Kodak, a 130-year-old company, an iconic brand, that had just filed for bankruptcy having failed to adapt to the digital era.

'People also have to adapt,' she said to me over dinner at a Japanese restaurant off Sunset. 'You either get with technology or you don't. Look at Kodak. Adapt or die. Fuck, you live your life on Facebook anyway.'

She wasn't far wrong.

When I got unexpectedly rebuffed in bed after we'd spent a wonderful day walking around Santa Monica, I broke down and cried. It wasn't about the sex. Rather it felt like it was all over. I wanted love more than anything but realised then with Tori that it wasn't ever going to happen. The emotion spilled out of me like water from a tap. I was embarrassed.

Tori's response was pure indignation. Not reading how I was feeling at all, she totally lost it.

'What am I? Your fucking *whore*?'

I didn't know who this person was. She wasn't the person I'd expected to meet. There was pain inside her. There was still pain inside me, too, but I had let most of it out. I was open to her and *being* open to her. To the possibility of making something from the short time we had together. But it felt like she wasn't open on any level to me.

'Sometimes, Tori, you just have to take a chance and "let the right one in".'

She'd recently watched the Swedish horror movie of the same name. I thought the reference was clever.

'I think me inviting a stranger from Australia to stay in my apartment for two weeks is letting you in already, don't you?'

She switched off her bed light. I went out to the kitchen, turned on my computer and wrote her a letter on Facebook. That just about said it all. It was easier to type online in the next room what I had to say to her than it was to wake her up and do it right to her face. It hit me then. I'd had unrealistic expectations of the whole thing. I'd been sentenced to another term of disconnected love. When I'd finished I made a Skype call to Evie. Jarringly, a picture of Lara's boyfriend, Wes, came up as the avatar on my ex-wife's account. Sans shirt. *Nice.*

Lara answered the call and came into the frame, smiling, beautiful as always. I felt incredibly sad. I was looking from the other side of the world not just at the wife I'd lost but the life I'd lost. Yet she was looking at me in this Hollywood apartment with the glamorous non-girlfriend asleep in the next room as if I was the lucky one.

The fact was we'd both missed out.

When the sun came up the next morning I went up to the roof with its expansive views of the hills, a 'double cappuccino without the foam' in my hand. Tori stayed asleep in bed. I scanned the urban bustle stretching in all directions and was struck by some incongruous paint-rollered graffiti on a building near Fairfax and Melrose. From where I was standing, the size of it was enormous. A plaintive cry in the romantic moor of LA. Just two words in bright red on a background of cream.

LOVE ME

How I wished someone would.

* * *

The following weekend Tori and I were invited to a Superbowl party at Renée Zellweger's house in Santa Monica. The fact that the Oscar-winning actress was another ex of Bradley Cooper didn't escape me.

Other faces were familiar. TV stars. Film directors. Models. Rockstars. A bunch of TV comedians, all male, all brilliant but obnoxious, cracking open crummy American beers and trying their best to out-amuse each other. But rather than mingle and network I spent most of the time distressed that I was losing Tori or didn't even have her in the first place.

LET THE RIGHT ONE IN

One minute I'd been at Piazzolla admitting to a bunch of guys I fucked a sofa. The next I was in the kitchen of Bridget Jones, looking askance as nearby a world-ranked cage fighter with a shaved head and latissimus dorsi like swinging locker doors put moves on the stunning woman I'd arrived with. He knew we were 'together' but simply didn't give a fuck. Tori, for her part, had drunk too much wine to notice the turmoil I was in. Not being a couple officially or otherwise, and not knowing how Tori felt about me, I didn't feel right about confronting him. I was at a *party*, in any case. So I went out onto the porch and fell into a conversation with a wisecracking TV and film director called Phil who could have been the long-lost brother of Sydney Pollack. He'd worked with Heath Ledger and liked Aussies.

We talked about our marriages and our divorces. How it felt to contemplate suicide. That feeling of not wanting to die but just for someone to notice the pain we were in. He was directing a movie about a man and a woman who meet when they're both about to kill themselves but go on to become lovers and rediscover their joy for life in the process. I told him my sad, sorry story.

'Wait, my Aussie friend. Say again? He got your *dog*?'

When I went back inside the cage-fighting cockblocker was going in hard, touching Tori's face, asking for her number. He refused to acknowledge my presence, even when

I walked up to stand next to her. In my mind I pictured myself throwing a spectacular hook but this was a flat-nosed Orc who pulverised people for a living. I hadn't even been able to fend off David's elbows.

He handed her his iPhone. She keyed in her number. I couldn't believe what I was seeing.

'I've known him for years. It's no big deal,' she said when I got a chance to speak with her alone. 'There's no way I would consider him for something long term.'

Long term.

The two words winded me like a short, sharp jab to the stomach. I walked off. I didn't know whether to stay or leave. There was a chair by the fireplace in the living room. I could hide away there. So I did. After about 15 minutes, feeling like my soul was about to implode, Tori found me again.

'Have you been here the whole time?'

'Yes.'

'What's wrong?'

'I feel terrible.'

'I'm sorry.'

'I can't believe you gave that guy your number.'

I'd said too much. She had her back up. It was like something had gone off in her head.

'You think I gave him my number because I want to fuck *him*? That guy? You are kidding me. You think I'm a *whore*?

You think I would do that? You know what? Fuck you. It didn't mean anything. It's nothing.'

'You said you wouldn't consider him for something long term. Nothing about short term.'

'What? What are you talking about? Long term, short term, I wouldn't consider him for *anything*.'

I was totally confused. She offered to leave but I knew if I agreed it was well and truly over between us. Maybe I'd got it all wrong. I was still clinging to hope. So we stayed and Tori went outside to play running charades with Renée, the UFC arsehole and a bunch of others on the back lawn. I excused myself by pretending to have jet lag but in truth I was just heartbroken.

When the game was over, I got chatting with Renée by the fridge. She was washing dishes. A tiny woman. Completely lovely. She made a joke at her own expense while having some trouble separating the rubbish from the recycling.

'This is the reason why none of my relationships ever last. My boyfriends didn't care about recycling.'

It struck me I might have been better off trying my luck with Bridget Jones.

'So you're from Australia, Jesse. Which part?'

'Sydney.'

'Which part of Sydney?'

'Darlinghurst.'

'Oh, I know Darlinghurst very well. Great place. My dad grew up in Cronulla. So what brings you all the way out here?'

'I came for a woman.'

'Well, you've got a pretty amazing one right there.'

The problem, of course, was that I didn't have her. I had a fat load of nothing all over again.

* * *

The drive back from Santa Monica to West Hollywood was awful. Tori wouldn't speak to me. She just plugged her iPhone into the car stereo and turned on the internet radio station Pandora. All while texting. The infernal device should have been surgically grafted into her left wrist. Who was she texting all the time? What was she saying about me? I couldn't help feeling paranoid.

Adapt or die.

When we got back to her apartment we got into bed and I unloaded on her again about what had happened at the party. She was listening but somewhere else.

'What's going on, Tori?'

'I have to process a lot of stuff. It's got nothing to do with you.'

'It's got everything to do with me. I'm here. I came halfway across the world to be with you. I care about you more than you know. I fucking adore you. I want to be the man you need in your life. And you need one, Tori. You've got to let me in.'

'I'm not ready to share those things with you. I don't know you.'

'What do you mean you don't know me? I've spent every day thinking about you. Waiting to come here. Starving myself to look good for you. Running twice a day. Working towards nothing else. You've got to give more. I love you.'

As soon as I said it I knew it was a lie. I didn't. This wasn't anywhere near real. But I *wanted* to love Tori. I had to *do* something.

'I know you do.'

And with those frigid words she turned away, as she had every night since I'd got to LA, and went to sleep on her side of the bed.

* * *

The next evening Tori and I went to another party, this time in Beachwood Canyon at a house built by Howard Hughes for one of his mistresses and owned by two screenwriters. A gay couple. They wrote movies together. Romantic comedies. One stayed outside, smoked pot and came up with the ideas, the other stayed inside and banged away at the

Mac. They fucked. Got away to their cabin in the woods on weekends. And came back and did it all again. They had it all worked out. The perfect relationship. Seemingly, anyway.

Why couldn't I have one?

'I just feel unbearable pressure to fall in love with you, Jesse,' Tori finally admitted on the drive home. 'You're a great guy and I'm open to this but right now you're a weight on me.'

I was doing the same thing to her I had with Lara and Frankie. Wanting it too much. Going too fast. Overcompensating.

'I'm sorry, Tori. I've fucked up.'

'No, you haven't fucked up at all. It's just I don't want to feel the pressure of time or "one week left" because I feel like that sets us up for failure. I want to feel excited about getting to know you and instead it feels like a chore. It's just so heavy. If you think I'm going to tell you I'm in love with you at the airport it's not going to happen. I can't say what's going to happen between us. But I know right now I'm not in love with you.'

'And I'm not in love with you.'

She smiled at me. 'And that's fine.'

'This genie's going back into the bottle.'

'Don't be so dramatic. I'll be here. I see all this as the beginning. Who knows what the future holds? I'm not going anywhere.'

But I was going home. The pressure off, just like with Olivia in Boston, we had the best sex of the whole trip when we got back to her apartment. I felt we connected, even without the true intimacy I missed so much.

Perhaps my philandering past had got her spooked that I wasn't in it for the right reasons, that she was just another notch on my bedpost. I couldn't turn back the clock and change what I'd done. I was paying for that. Equally, though, if it had just been the 'beginning' for her, I shouldn't have travelled halfway across the world to lie in her bed. We were both to blame. But it came down to one thing in the end: I had wanted it too much.

When Tori fell asleep I answered some emails and found myself giving IM advice to Nina, a book publisher I'd met online and added on Facebook. She lived in New York. A 'friends' list is essentially a single man's reserves bench.

'I'll be going home single, waking up single, getting through the day single, wondering why the fuck I'm on this planet single all over again,' I said. 'My only identity is being a dad. When I'm in love with someone I feel like a whole person. Most of the time I feel like half a man. That's the truth.'

'Being a dad, a friend and a writer isn't a man? That is like three men rolled into one. I feel like you're not far from finding the love you want because you want it badly, and that's really important. Happiness is a choice. I just think some people are more focused on it than others.'

'Maybe you're right. I don't know what to think anymore.'

'Last week I met this guy online. We went on a date and after about ten or 15 minutes I realised I really liked him. He was hot – good job, funny, smart, manly but not too manly, very well dressed. So what did I do? Like an idiot I ate nothing, drank too much sake, got loaded, went back to his place and fucked him three times, did the walk of shame in the morning and beat myself up over it. How could I want love so badly, and be so picky, and when I find someone seemingly just right, fuck it up so royally?'

'What do you mean, "fuck it up"? How?'

'I can't help thinking if I'd just gone home after the sake, it'd be different. I'd have seen him again. It's been a week. We've texted each other but he's unavailable. My therapist says, "When a guy shows you he has limited availability, believe him." Sometimes I get so much anxiety about never finding a life partner, I can't even sleep. So, compared to mine, your experience has at least been much more graceful and rewarding.'

'You fucked him three times and you say that like it's bad thing. I don't get that.'

'Would you have lost respect for me?'

'No, I wouldn't have lost respect for you. It comes down to one simple thing with men: does he want to fuck you for the rest of his life and does he think he can do any better? Why's he unavailable?'

'Busy with work. But wants to hang out again. Last message was: "Have a great week!"'

'*Hang out?* Code for "fuck without obligation".'

'In New York, men are incredibly aloof.'

'Because they're keeping their options open, Nina. He's not into you. Just as Tori's not into me. If he likes you he likes you. Men are men everywhere.'

'Yep.'

'Some are just bigger fools than others.'

* * *

I was down on the losing end again. But I was starting to see myself clearly.

My friends thought I was having the time of my life from what they could see on Facebook: the photos of me and Tori looking like a couple. They didn't know how I really felt, which was to log off and shut down the fucking thing forever. To turn my back on all of them. I'd had it with not just being disconnected in relationships and with my family but from myself. The man I used to be. The one who read three books a week and not three books a year, if I was lucky. The one who researched for hours in libraries and not for a couple of minutes on Google. Fucking internet.

As for luck, it had run out along with my money. Chance, too, once my friend, was playing tricks on me. Tori and I went to a Chinese massage place on Sunset where we sat down in adjoining chairs. I looked down and there between us was the November 28, 2011 edition of *People* magazine with Bradley Cooper on the cover. The words "THE SEXIEST MAN ALIVE!", in bright yellow capitals, taunted me like a big fat playground bully.

As if she or I needed the reminder.

There was anguish because I had staked so much in coming to LA, but in truth it was almost a relief to let it go. The glimpse never came. I didn't get the Hollywood ending. All I got was me. But that, of course, was all I'd ever had and all I ever would have.

Only now, though, was I finally waking up to that immutable truth.

CHAPTER 16

BETTER MAN

TRACK 16 'Once in a Lifetime', Talking Heads, *Remain in Light* (1980)

Losing's a valuable part of life. Hurting. Fucking up. Feeling like you're going to end it. That's what I'd learned since Lara left me on the end of that bed in Enfield. With love, you have to put yourself in a position to win but accept the chance you will fail. But that's what so many people don't do. They just settle and refuse to countenance failure. They vaccinate themselves against risk. Eliminate chance. Like turning down the dark street. Or drinking the 86/100 wine. Or going to the badly reviewed restaurant. Or reading the book with the hideous cover. Dating, even marrying, the 'wrong' people when they might just turn out to be right.

In my 20s I set myself up as the winner. The guy with the perfect wife. The perfect kid. The perfect job. I had it all. And then came the fall. I lost my wife. My family. My house. My savings. My career. My dog. My mind. I never got a chance at reconciliation. I didn't get back the chance of making something whole again with Lara or with Frankie. But what I had was whole enough.

I often think back to how Evie got through the first week of her life when her foramen ovale, the little flap in her heart, hadn't closed up properly. She had fluid on her lungs, doctors were talking about clicky hips; the bad news wouldn't end. In the neonatal ward at Royal Prince Alfred Hospital in Sydney, sitting beside her humidicrib, wanting desperately to hold her, I looked around at the other sick babies, including a boy who was in a critical condition. He was being kept alive only by a cobweb of tubes and wires, and had been there so long his parents had had to return home to work some 500 kilometres away. He was the size of an eggplant.

I realised then that Evie was one of the lucky ones. When I finally got to touch her, one of her little red index fingers hooked around mine, I knew I could never let her go. And, as much as I'd tried to escape from my pain all through her short life, I hadn't.

In childbirth the likelihood of something going wrong is very high. It's no different with falling in love. We do anything for our children and love them even when they annoy the hell out of us. But we don't do the same for our relationships. They don't end up in a neonatal ward. Somewhere along the line we have lost that unbreakable commitment to nurturing romantic love when the glimpses start to close up. We've lost patience with it because we've lost patience with everything else. It can all be thrown away. Our gadgets. Our clothes. Our pets. Our film stars. Our kitchens. Our furniture. Even our homes aren't bought to be actually *lived* in. They're bought to be sold. To be profited from so we can upgrade.

Isn't it time we all stopped upgrading?

* * *

I flew back to Australia after saying goodbye to Tori at the airport. It was a strange charade, as such moments often are, going in for a hug and promising we'd stay in touch but both knowing it was the last time we'd see each other. On the plane I had a lot of time to think, to do what Tori had been doing while I'd been in California: *processing*. I wasn't looking forward to walking into Piazzolla and getting ribbed by the Darlinghurst Council of Elders after having built my LA woman into something she was not, but it came with the territory. Their barbs were always affectionate, never cruel. They were my friends and wanted the best for me. And I wasn't about to make excuses to them or anyone else. I didn't ever want to be a man who stopped hoping for love or stopped looking for that glimpse. Sure I'd made some mistakes, big ones, but I was gaining some clarity and coming to terms with my faults: the baggage, the temper, the demands I placed on other people – physical and emotional – while not always meeting their expectations myself.

When I picked up Evie from school that day and saw the joy on her face as she ran up to embrace me, it hit me that I'd been carried across the Pacific on a tradewind of hopeful fantasy. The love I felt for my daughter was real. There was nothing disconnected or forced. It was unconditional. Almost nine, on the edge of adolescence, she was the true love of my life and always would be – wherever I ended up.

'Oh, Daddy, I missed you *soooo* much,' she said, downloading all her news about her friends and what movies she'd seen since I'd been away and neglecting to ask after Tori. She knew the score when it came to her father and his romantic hit-and-runs.

'We'll still go to Disneyland, I promise, Evie. It might just take a little bit longer to get there, okay?'

'Cool. Dad, can I sleep in your bed tonight? *Please.*'

Asleep in her pyjamas, clutching the stuffed Big Bird she'd had since we'd first arrived in Darlinghurst, I turned on my laptop and reactivated the same dating profile I'd used first to meet Sunny and then Tori. Fuck it. I wasn't going to change overnight and I didn't want to. I loved women. I loved being in love. And I wasn't going to give up trying to find The One who was looking for me too. It wasn't Lara. It wasn't Frankie. She was out there. I just didn't know where.

An early candidate emerged within days. Natalie, a 42-year-old personal trainer in, of all places, West Hollywood.

'You were down the damn street from me!' she shrieked when I told her I'd just come back from the States with my tail between my legs. 'I would have spooned the bejesus out of you!'

I allowed myself a smile. Relationships live and die by the smallest margins. Your life can change on one simple decision. A single turn. Those sliding doors.

From wanting to slash myself with a kitchen knife at 34 and end it all, I was almost 40 and excited about living each and every day like it was my last.

How did I get here?

I'm still not sure, but I had to go through it all to get stripped back to what I am now and will remain: a man laid bare. But a resilient and hopeful one. And a better one.

I did my best to roll with the changes. Had some adventures. Met some incredible people. Made lifelong friends. And returned to the love of my daughter and the love of myself.

The most important glimpse of all.

SOUNDTRACK

TRACK 1 'Losin' End', Written by Michael McDonald, The Doobie Brothers, *Takin' It to the Streets*, Warner Bros (1976)

TRACK 2 'Lyin' Eyes', Written by Don Henley & Glenn Frey, Eagles, *One of These Nights*, Asylum (1975)

TRACK 3 'Tie You Up (The Pain of Love)', Written by Mick Jagger & Keith Richards, The Rolling Stones, *Undercover*, Rolling Stones/Virgin (1983)

TRACK 4 'Sting Me', Written by Chris Robinson & Rich Robinson, The Black Crowes, *The Southern Harmony and Musical Companion*, Def American (1992)

TRACK 5 'Way Down Now', Written by Karl Wallinger, World Party, *Goodbye Jumbo*, Papillon (1990)

TRACK 6 'Fire Woman', Written by Ian Astbury & Billy Duffy, The Cult, *Sonic Temple*, Beggars Banquet (1989)

LAID BARE

TRACK 7 'Amoreena', Written by Elton
John & Bernie Taupin, Elton John,
Tumbleweed Connection, DJM (1970)

TRACK 8 'Rock 'n' Roll Damnation', Written
by Angus Young, Malcolm Young & Bon
Scott, AC/DC, *Powerage*, Atlantic (1978)

TRACK 9 'Hot Legs', Written by Gary Grainger
& Rod Stewart, Rod Stewart, *Foot Loose
& Fancy Free*, Warner Bros (1977)

TRACK 10 'Buckets of Rain', Written by Bob Dylan,
Bob Dylan, *Blood on the Tracks*, Columbia (1975)

TRACK 11 'Mandolin Rain', Written by Bruce
Hornsby & John Hornsby, Bruce Hornsby and
the Range, *The Way It Is*, RCA (1986)

TRACK 12 'Cold as Ice', Written by Lou Gramm &
Mick Jones, Foreigner, *Foreigner*, Atlantic (1977)

TRACK 13 'Landed', Written by Ben Folds, Ben
Folds, *Songs for Silverman*, Epic (2005)

SOUNDTRACK

TRACK 14 'Welcome to the Club', Written by Joe Walsh, Joe Walsh, *So What*, ABC (1974)

TRACK 15 'Paradise City', Written by Axl Rose, Duff McKagan, Izzy Stradlin, Slash & Steven Adler, Guns N' Roses, *Appetite for Destruction*, Geffen (1987)

TRACK 16 'Once in a Lifetime', Written by David Byrne, Brian Eno, Chris Frantz, Jerry Harrison & Tina Weymouth, Talking Heads, *Remain in Light*, Sire (1980)

ACKNOWLEDGMENTS

This book wouldn't have been possible and I most likely wouldn't be here were it not for so many of the brilliant people who appear under pseudonyms in the preceding pages: Giancarlo, Enrico, Ron, Kristin, Gully, Sunny, Marguerite, the Darlinghurst Council of Elders and all the others ... you know who you are. You gave me true friendship, empathy and ballast when I needed it most. Your presence in my life means everything to me.

Those I can name deserve a mention: Aaron Caddy, Adrian Naimo, Alison Dines, Amy Janowski, Ana Kypreos, Andrew Jennings, Anthony Siokos, Bonita Mersiades, Cameron Fink, Carole Lloyd, Chris Wang, Chris Tanner, Christine Hazelton, Christophe Beaulieu, Claire Clements, Cleo Race, Col Fink, Cynthia Popper, Daniel and Miriam Feiler, Davidde Corran, David W. Larkin, Dawn McDaniel, Elizabeth Mazzocchi, Erin Rae Vasek, Gerald Gallagher, Giovanni Mele, Grace Cassio, Haki Dalan, Hayden Tyndall, Ian Griffiths, James Corbett, Jason Dasey, John Duerden, John Kellett, Joseph Carrano, Josh Folden, Karen Soo, Kellie Farr, Kelly Durant, Kirsty O'Shea, Kylie O'Brien, Lara Paonessa, Leo Karis, Leonardo Urbinati, Lou Nesci,

ACKNOWLEDGMENTS

Lou Sticca, Luke Benedictus, Marcelo Garrao, Marco Beraldo, Mario Szücs, Mark Stewart, Martin Warren, Matthew Thompson, Meika Aspland, Mel Poyner, Micheál Lovett, Mike Tuckerman, Molly Tait, Nadenna Natale, Neely Shearer, Netta Williams, Nia and Dennis Mothoneos, Neil Venkataramiah, Nicky Taylor, Oliver Fowler, Patrick Mangan, Pete Learmonth, Peter Kypreos, Peter Scott, Pim Verbeek, Ray Gatt, Richard Learmonth, Rod and Tegan Morrison, Scotty Gooding, Simon Harvey, Stephanie Howard, Taku Kimura, Thang Luong, Thomas Jane, Tina Cullen, Tom Donald, Tom Ferson, Tom Seungmin Lee, Umberto Megu, Vincenzo Sposato, Vladimir Cherepanoff, Wayne Shennen and Will Swanton.

Laid Bare had its genesis in an 800-word story I did for Australian *marie claire* magazine back in September 2011 on how it feels when your wife leaves you. I want to thank Genevieve Roth and Naomi Jaul for commissioning that story and express my sincere appreciation to all the women around Australia who wrote such kind and touching letters to me after it was published. To those of you out there who got the 'I love you but I'm not in love with you' speech from their wives or husbands, just know you're never alone.

Special thanks also to publisher Vanessa Radnidge, national accounts manager Daniel Pilkington, marketing manager Robert Watkins, publicity manager Judy Jamieson-

Green, publishing consultant Airlie Lawson and publishing director Fiona Hazard at Hachette Australia for their courage, unflappable positivity and belief in the book; to the editor, Jacquie Brown, for a sensitive but exacting edit; to the typesetter, Graeme Jones, for making the words look beautiful; to the designer, Christa Moffitt, for a great cover; to Michael McDonald and Bon Scott for uplifting me with their songs during a dark period of my life; and to Stephen Vizinczey for inspiration.

I owe a debt of gratitude to my sister and brothers, my brother-in-law, my stepmother and especially my parents. I hope my love for you both comes through in these pages. Sorry it didn't work for the two of you but, as you say, Mum, life's a series of letting go.

Lastly, to Lara and Frankie, I have recounted events through the lens of my own experience. Thank you for showing me those glimpses of eternity.

If you need help or someone to talk to about your troubles, you can contact:

Lifeline – 131114
Suicide Call Back Service – 1300 659 467
MensLine Australia – 1300 78 99 78
Kids Helpline – 1800 55 1800

SANE Australia can provide fact sheets on mental illness as well as advice on how to access treatment.

Visit www.sane.org or call 1800 18 SANE (7263).

You can also visit **beyondblue**: the national depression initiative (1300 22 4636) or the Black Dog Institute.

You can also talk to your local GP or health professional.